SCADA: Supervisory Control and Data Acquisition

2nd Edition

SCADA: Supervisory Control and Data Acquisition
2nd Edition

By Stuart A. Boyer
Iliad Engineering Inc.

ISA
67 Alexander Drive
P.O. Box 12277
Research Triangle Park
North Carolina 27709

Library of Congress Cataloging-in-Publication Data

Boyer, Stuart A.
    SCADA : supervisory control and data acquisition / by Stuart A.
    Boyer.
        p.   cm.
    Includes bibliographical references (p.   ) and index.
    ISBN 1-55617-660-0
    1. Management information systems—Programmed instruction.
    2. Supervisory control systems—Programmed instruction.
    3. Automatic data collection systems—Programmed instruction.
    I. Title.
    T58.6.B675   1999
    670.42'75—dc21   98-52774
                                                                        CIP

TABLE OF CONTENTS

Preface to the Second Edition

When the first edition of this book was written, certain trends in SCADA were already apparent, and I made attempts to identify them in Unit 14, "What's Next?" Generally, these trends have continued; however, some of them have moved more quickly than I expected at that time. This edition will therefore address, hopefully in a seamless way, some of the changes in technology that have occurred.

Since the first edition was published, several software products have been developed that are called "SCADA" packages. It is important for the reader of this book to be aware that while these software products may be incorporated as parts of a SCADA system, the definition of SCADA used in this book is much broader than the definition used by the manufacturers of these software packages.

This book forms the basis of a two-day course offered by ISA. Questions generated in these classes have resulted in the expansion of certain parts of this edition.

ISA's Independent Learning Modules

This book is an Independent Learning Module (ILM) as developed and published by ISA. The ILMs are the principal components of a major educational system designed primarily for independent self-study. This comprehensive learning system has been custom designed and created for ISA to more fully educate people in the basic theories and technologies associated with applied instrumentation and control.

The ILM system is divided into several distinct sets of modules on closely related topics. Each such set of individually related modules is called a "series." The ILM system is composed of the ISA series of modules on the following topics:

- control principles and techniques
- fundamental instrumentation
- unit process and unit operation control
- professional development
- specific industries
- software-associated topics

The principal components of the series are the individual ILMs (or modules), such as this book. Because they are especially designed for independent self-study, no other text or references are required. The unique format, style, and teaching techniques employed in the ILMs make them a powerful addition to any library. The ILMs that have been published thus far are as follows:

Application Concepts of Process Control by Paul W. Murrill (1988)

Continuous Control Techniques for Distributed Control Systems by Gregory K. McMillan (1989)

Computer Control Strategies for the Fluid Process Industries by Albert A. Gunkler and John W. Bernard (1990)

Tuning of Industrial Control Systems by Armando B. Corripio (1990)

Fundamentals of Process Control Theory, second edition, by Paul W. Murrill (1991)

Conceptual Design Analysis Applied to Offshore Control Systems by Bill G. Tompkins (1992)

Environmental Control Systems by Randy D. Down (1992)

The Management of Control Systems: Justification and Technical Auditing by N. E. Battikha (1992)

Flow Control by W. S. Buzzard (1994)

pH Measurement and Control, second edition, by Gregory K. McMillan (1994)

Advanced Temperature Control by G. K. McMillan and C. M. Toarmina (1995)

Economics of Control Improvement by P. G. Friedmann (1995)

Smart Sensors by P. Chapman (1996)

Measurement Uncertainty: Methods and Applications, second edition, by Ronald H. Dieck (1997)

SCADA: Supervisory Control and Data Acquisition, second edition, by Stuart A. Boyer (1999)

This series should be a foundational part of any professional library in instrumentation and control.

Paul W. Murrill
Consulting Editor, ILM Series

Comments on this Volume

Certain processes cover areas that may be measured in the thousands of square miles and have dimensions that may be hundreds, occasionally thousands, of miles long.Over the past thirty years, a method known as SCADA, for supervisory control and data acquisition, has evolved for monitoring and controlling processes that cover such large areas. As with most evolving technologies, SCADA has borrowed something from one applied science and something else from others. It is now a mature technology. That is not to say that SCADA will stop evolving but rather that most of its current techniques have cleared the hurdles that the real world places in the path of new ideas.

This Independent Learning Module was developed to provide the reader with an understanding of the technology known as SCADA.

Dedication

I would like to dedicate this book to Linda, who has provided both practical and moral support in its development, even though—or perhaps because—neither of us understood at the beginning how much work would be involved.

Stuart A. Boyer

Unit 1:
Introduction and Overview

UNIT 1

Introduction and Overview

Welcome to the ISA's Independent Learning Module (ILM) on SCADA (supervisory control and data acquisition). This unit provides an overview of the course and the information you will need for independent study.

Learning Objectives — When you have completed this unit, you should:

A. Know the nature of the material in the course.

B. Understand the general organization of the material.

C. Know the course objectives.

1-1. Course Coverage

This course provides introductory technical material about SCADA systems. It addresses the basic layout of SCADA systems and the parameters for process selection. Communications and the basic building blocks of SCADA systems are dealt with in greater detail. A discussion of economic tools and future trends rounds out the course.

No recommendations about specific equipment or methods are provided although techniques that enable the reader to make such selections are included.

1-2. Purpose

The purpose of this ILM is to introduce the student to the basics of SCADA by providing overviews of relevant topics where possible and details where necessary. Since SCADA consists of the elements of several different technologies, it is sometimes difficult to know where to stop when describing some of these technologies to the reader. The course attempts to focus on such technologies to the extent that they make SCADA more understandable. The course also identifies major differences between the SCADA systems of different industries. Because the basics of SCADA are much the same from one industry to another, however, examples from many industries have been included throughout the course.

1-3.   Audience and Prerequisites

This ILM is designed for those who wish to learn the basics of SCADA by themselves at their own pace. It is designed to be useful to managers, supervisors, engineers, operators, and technicians who contemplate coming in contact with SCADA systems. It will also be useful to students of technical schools and colleges as an introduction to the subject. To any technical people who have a personal interest, it should also serve as a source of overview information about SCADA.

1-4.   Study Materials

This text is the only study material required. It is one of ISA's Independent Learning Modules systems. As such, it is designed as an independent, stand-alone textbook that is uniquely and specifically structured for self-study. For better understanding, the student may find it helpful to study ILMs on related subjects. A list of ILMs is located in the preface to this book on page x.

1-5.   Organization and Sequence

This ILM is divided into fourteen separate units. Unit 2 is an overview of SCADA, which provides some definitions and discusses some of SCADA's limitations. It should focus the student's attention on those factors that make SCADA what it is. Unit 3 provides a sketch of the history of the technology and defines it in the context of related technologies. Units 4 and 5 discuss the importance of data currency ("How up to date is the information?") and describe how this data currency is used to select what process functions can be addressed by SCADA.

Units 6 and 7 concern the transfer of information between the remote field location and the master or central location. While several communications media are available, radio is probably the most common one for SCADA. For this reason, and because radio has some limitations that other media do not have, an entire unit (Unit 7) is devoted to it. Units 8 and 9 describe the hardware. The "black box"--the RTU (remote terminal unit)--is discussed in Unit 8; the MTU (master terminal unit) is explained in some detail in Unit 9.

The end devices and the auxiliary equipment at the process end of the communications link are presented in Unit 10. Individual sensors, actuators, and signal conditioners are relatively inexpensive, but because there are so many of them in a SCADA system their combined purchase, installation, and maintenance cost may exceed the cost of all the more complex elements. Unit 11 identifies some of the applications for which

SCADA is used. It points out that at present SCADA systems are used much more for remote control than for automatic control. Some cautions are voiced in this unit to avoid applications that would be weakened by the natural limitations of SCADA. Different industries have developed SCADA in subtly different directions. Unit 11 will identify some of these differences.

Unit 12 discusses how the operator receives information from and sends information to the system. The SCADA operator interface is a technological field that has ridden on the shoulders of several other operator interface technologies. Our industrial success depends on making sound economic and implementation decisions. The factors to consider when evaluating SCADA projects form the subject of Unit 13. Unit 14 projects SCADA into the future, based on trends in both operations and the technology. It is useful--even necessary--to try to imagine what SCADA will be doing in the future so the systems currently being planned will have longer useful lives.

Appendixes A and B provide references for further reading and definitions of acronyms and specialty words, respectively. As with most electronics-based technologies, SCADA is a virtual cornucopia of these terms and abbreviations. Finally, the solutions to the exercises found at the end of each unit are given in Appendix C.

1-6.   Course Objectives

When you have completed this entire ILM, you should be able to do the following:

A. Be conversant with SCADA nomenclature.

B. Describe the typical architecture of a SCADA system.

C. Understand the basic technology of each of SCADA's major building blocks.

D. Understand the limitations of SCADA.

E. Understand when a SCADA system would be beneficial to your operation.

F. Select the appropriate SCADA technologies for your operational requirements.

In addition to these general objectives, each unit contains a specific set of learning objectives to help direct your study in that unit.

1-7.   Course Length

The basic idea of the ISA system of ILMs is that students learn best if they proceed at their own personal pace. As a result, the amount of time individual students will require to complete this ILM will vary significantly. However, most students will complete this course in eighteen hours.

Unit 2:
What Is SCADA?

UNIT 2

What Is SCADA?

SCADA is the technology that enables a user to collect data from one or more distant facilities and/or send limited control instructions to those facilities. SCADA makes it unnecessary for an operator to be assigned to stay at or frequently visit remote locations when those remote facilities are operating normally. SCADA includes the operator interface and the manipulation of application-related data--but it is not limited to that. Some manufacturers are building software packages that they call SCADA, and while these are often well suited to act as parts of a SCADA system, because they lack communications links and other necessary equipment they are not complete SCADA systems.

This unit discusses some of the processes that can benefit from the installation of SCADA, introduces the basic elements of the SCADA system, and notes some of the benefits that the system can provide.

Learning Objectives — When you have completed this unit, you should:

A. Have a general understanding of how SCADA is used.

B. Know the elements of a SCADA system.

C. Understand the terms that describe subsystems.

D. Recognize types of processes that could benefit from SCADA.

2-1. Definition of SCADA

SCADA is an acronym that is formed from the first letters of the term "supervisory control and data acquisition." Aside from the fact that the root term does not refer to the factor of distance, which is common to most SCADA systems, the acronym SCADA is a good one. It rhymes with "Raid ah."

A SCADA system allows an operator to make set point changes on distant process controllers, to open or close valves or switches, to monitor alarms, and to gather measurement information from a location central to a widely distributed process, such as an oil or gas field, pipeline system, or hydroelectric generating complex. When the dimensions of the process become very large—hundreds or even thousands of kilometers from one end to the others—one can appreciate the benefits SCADA offers in terms of reducing the cost of routine visits to monitor facility operation. The value of these benefits will grow even more if the facilities are very remote and require extreme effort (e.g., a helicopter trip) to visit.

2-2. Applicable Processes

SCADA technology is best applied to processes that are spread over large areas; are relatively simple to control and monitor; and require frequent, regular, or immediate intervention. The following examples of such processes should help you visualize the range of application types SCADA is suitable for:

A. Groups of small hydroelectric generating stations that are turned on and off in response to customer demand are usually located in remote locations, they can be controlled by opening and closing valves to the turbine, they must be monitored continuously, and they need to respond relatively quickly to demands on the electric power grid.

B. Oil or gas production facilities—including wells, gathering systems, fluid measurement equipment, and pumps—are usually spread over large areas, require relatively simple controls such as turning motors on and off, need to gather meter information regularly, and must respond quickly to conditions in the rest of the field.

C. Pipelines for gas, oil, chemicals, or water have elements that are located at varying distances from a central control point, can be controlled by opening and closing valves or starting and stopping pumps, and must be capable of responding quickly to market conditions and to leaks of dangerous or environmentally sensitive materials.

D. Electric transmission systems may cover thousands of square kilometers, can be controlled by opening and closing switches, and must respond almost immediately to load changes on the lines.

E. Irrigation systems often cover hundreds of square miles, can be controlled by opening and closing simple valves, and require the gathering of meter values for the water supplied to consumers.

These examples are just that—examples. SCADA has been successfully installed on each of these types of processes as well as many others. The types of control illustrated in these examples may give the mistaken impression that SCADA is not suitable for more complex control. As we will describe later, the complexity of remote control that is possible with SCADA has grown as the technology has matured.

Typical signals gathered from remote locations include alarms, status indications, analog values, and totalized meter values. However, a vast range of information can be gathered with this apparently limited menu of available signal types. More will be said about this in Unit 10. Similarly, signals sent from the SCADA's central location to the remote site are usually limited to discrete binary bit changes or to analog values addressed to a device at the process. An example of a binary bit change would be an instruction ordering a motor to stop. An example of an analog value would be an instruction to change a valve controller set point to 70 percent. Given simple signal types like these, with some imagination many control changes can be effected.

2-3. Elements of a SCADA System

Figure 2-1 shows the major components of a SCADA system. At the center is the operator, who accesses the system by means of an operator interface device, which is sometimes called "an operator console." The operator console functions as the operator's window into the process. It consists of a video display unit (VDU) that displays real-time data about the process and a keyboard for inputting the operator's commands or messages back to the process. Other cursor-positioning devices, such as a trackball, mouse, or touch screen may be used. If the system is very simple, it may be sufficient to have a set of annunciator windows that mimic the condition of the remote process. Often, an audible signal will be included.

The operator's input device is usually a computer keyboard, although pointing devices such as trackballs and mice are gaining in popularity. For very basic systems, a set of simple electrical switches may be sufficient. The operator interfaces with the master terminal unit (MTU), which is the system controller. Some industries use the term "host computer" instead of MTU. Throughout this book the two terms can be considered to be interchangeable. The MTU in modern SCADA systems is always based on a computer. It can monitor and control the field even when the operator is not present. It does this by means of a built-in scheduler that can be programmed to repeat instructions at set intervals. For example, it may be scheduled to request an update from each remote terminal unit (RTU) every six minutes. A more detailed description of the MTU is provided in Unit 9.

MTUs must communicate with RTUs that are located away from the central location. A SCADA system may have as few as one RTU or as many several hundred. There are two common media of communication, as shown in Figure 2-1: land line, which takes the form of optical fiber cable or electrical cable and is either owned by the company or leased from a telephone utility, and radio. In either case, a MODEM, which

MOdulates and DEModulates a signal on the carrier, is required. Some large systems may use a combination of radio and telephone lines for communication. One of the distinguishing features of SCADA systems is that their processes tend to be simple. For that reason, the amount of information moved over a SCADA system tends to be rather small, and, therefore, the data rate at which the modem works is also small. Often 300 bps (bits of information per second) is sufficient. Except for those used on electric utilities, few SCADA systems need to operate at data rates above 2400 bps. This allows voice-grade telephone lines to be used, and this bit rate does not overload most radio systems.

Normally, the MTU will have auxiliary devices (e.g., printers and backup memories) attached to it. These devices are considered to be part of the MTU. In many applications, the MTU is required to send accounting information to other computers or management information to other systems. These connections may be via dedicated cables between the MTU and the other computers, but in new SCADA systems they predominantly connect in the form of LAN (local area network) drops. In most SCADA systems, the MTU must also receive information from other computers. This is often how applications programs, operating on other computers and connected to the SCADA computer, provide a form of supervisory control over SCADA.

Figure 2-2 shows an RTU and its various connections. As mentioned, the RTUs communicate with the MTU by a modulated signal on cable or radio. Each RTU must have the capability to understand that a message has been directed to it, to decode the message, to act on the message, to respond if necessary, and to shut down to await a new message. Acting on the message may be a very complex procedure. It may require checking the present position of field equipment, comparing the existing position to the required position, sending an electrical signal to a field device that orders it to change states, checking a set of switches to ensure that the order was obeyed, and sending a message back to the MTU to confirm that the new condition has been reached. Because of this complexity, most RTUs are based on computer technology. The details of RTUs will be discussed in Unit 8.

The connections between the RTU and field devices are most often made with electrical conductors—that is, wires. Usually, the RTU supplies the electrical power for both sensors and low-power actuators. Depending on the process, reliability requirements may necessitate that an uninterruptible power supply (UPS) be used to ensure that failures of the electric utility do not result in process or safety upsets. This is particularly important if the SCADA system is installed on an electric utility system. The details of sensors will be discussed in Unit 10.

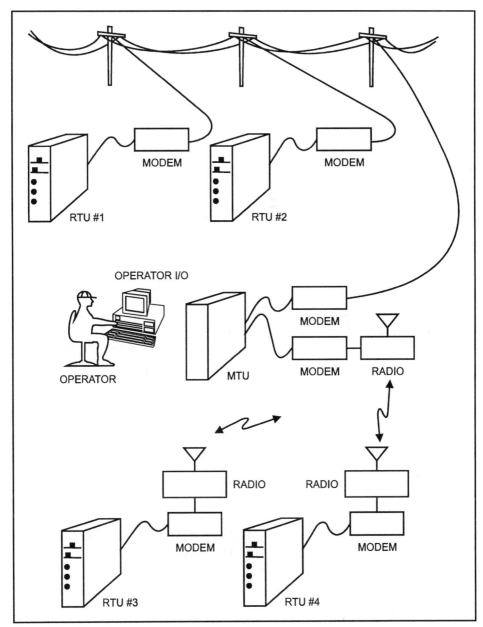

Figure 2-1. Major Components of a SCADA System

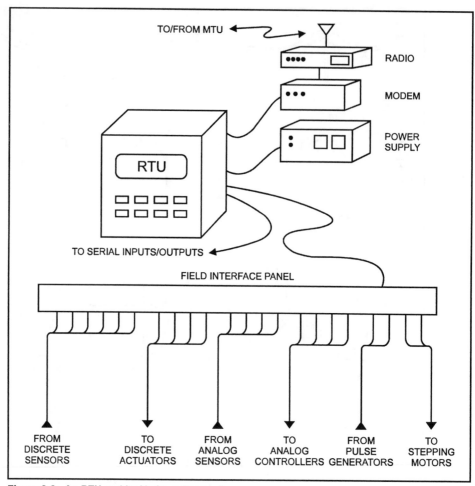

Figure 2-2. An RTU and Its Various Connections

Just as the MTU scans each RTU, the RTU scans each of the sensors and actuators that are wired into it. However, the RTU's scanning is done at a much higher scan rate than the scanning of the MTU.

2-4. A Two-way System

Although SCADA systems limit the amount of control that can be exercised from the MTU, they still do allow control. This is one of the things that distinguishes SCADA from most telemetry systems. SCADA is a two-way system. With SCADA, it is possible not only to monitor what is going on at a remote location but also to do something about it. The supervisory control part of SCADA takes care of that.

Exercises:

2-1. *What factor makes SCADA different from other control and monitoring systems?*

2-2. *Most SCADA systems operate at relatively low data rates. How does this affect the selection of communications equipment?*

2-3. *Name the three primary subsystems of a SCADA system.*

2-4. *Two communications media are frequently used with SCADA systems. What are they?*

2-5. *What three characteristics of processes make them potential candidates for SCADA?*

2-6. *In a process, the temperature of a heated liquid, the status of an open-close ball valve, and the number of cubic meters of gas that have passed through a meter must be gathered. Which can be gathered by a SCADA system?*

2-7. *From where do the process sensors receive their electrical energy?*

2-8. *Why is an uninterruptible power supply (UPS) needed at an RTU?*

Unit 3:
A Brief History
of SCADA

UNIT 3

A Brief History of SCADA

In learning a new subject, it is usually helpful to become acquainted with at least a small amount of its history. This enables you to place the new information in a context that is familiar. Knowing something about a subject's history also allows us to understand that subject in terms of its development over time. The better we can relate to the subject, the "friendlier" that subject becomes.

Learning Objectives — When you have completed this unit, you should:

A. Know the precursor technologies that contributed to SCADA.

B. Recognize the impact that radio and computer development have had on SCADA.

C. Appreciate how old the SCADA technology is.

3-1. Development from Telemetry

In the first two-thirds of the twentieth century, the engineering development of aircraft and rockets as well as the investigation of weather and other geophysical parameters required that simple pieces of data be gathered from equipment located where it was either difficult or impossible to staff observers. For example, in earlier days of experimental aviation aircraft had space for a pilot but little room left over for design and testing engineers to accompany the vehicle and monitor the hundreds of sensors installed to evaluate stresses and strains on the airframe and engine.

Similarly, early rockets did not even have room for a pilot, and, because all the early rocket trips ended very suddenly, it would have been difficult in any case to get engineers or technologists to volunteer to ride along to read the instruments! The fact that most of these early trips not only ended suddenly but much sooner than scheduled made it doubly necessary to find a way to get the flight information while it was still available. Obviously, in the early days of rocketry things were not going the way the designers had planned.

From the time technology was first applied to predicting weather, scientists realized that large masses of data would be required to make accurate forecasts. But only a very small amount of this data was available where people were generally located. Remote post offices and lighthouses, ships, and specially established weather stations could be manned and could transmit the data to a central location, either by telephone, telegraph, or radio. But that only accounted for surface information, and weather is composed of much more than surface effects. To get a better handle on weather, scientists thought that developing profiles of the weather information up through the atmosphere would be helpful. Small balloons were affordable. Small instruments could be mounted on them to measure the parameters of interest and provide the desired information. But how should that information be gathered?

The answer to this problem emerged from a communications method that was being used in another industry to alleviate a safety concern. For some time, rail systems had used wire communications to monitor the position of their rolling stock and the status of the switches that controlled the track on which the trains traveled. Figure 3-1 shows how this was accomplished using electric status switches, wire, and status lights. Very long distances required repeaters. This communications system, called telemetry, allowed a central office to monitor things that were happening at remote locations and enabled controllers to efficiently and safely schedule the trains. Instructions to manually change the position of the track switches would be sent by telegraph to operators. The system was, of course, limited to fixed facilities where wires could be laid between the source of the signal and the office in which the monitor worked. But where these conditions applied, telemetry worked well. Systems of this kind are still in use.

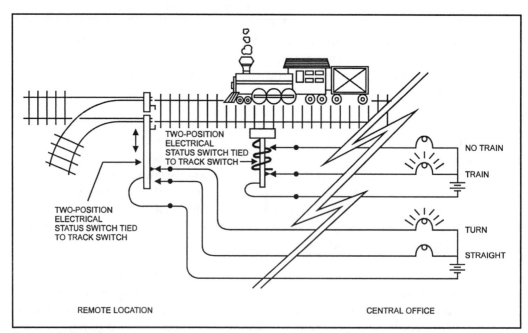

Figure 3-1. Early Telemetry

3-2.   Dependence on Communications and Computers

At about the same time that the need arose to maintain communications with moving facilities, radio technology was also advancing. As long as one didn't expect to get too much information, radio could send it. And as long as the radio didn't have to transmit for too long a time, its battery could be small enough to be practical. The technology of radio telemetry was thus born. Figure 3-2 outlines how a temperature sensor and a barometer could be tied to a radio to provide information about temperature and pressure versus altitude.

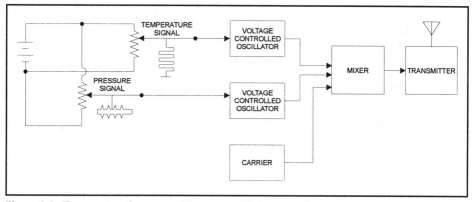

Figure 3-2. Temperature Sensor and Barometer Tied to a Radio

Radio telemetry evolved over time by improving the reliability of the radio system, by increasing the density of the data that could be transmitted, by developing error-detecting and even error-correcting codes, and by miniaturizing the equipment. But, generally speaking, radio telemetry continued for a long time as a one-way system; data was gathered from the remote site and transmitted to a central location. No radio signals were sent from the central location to the remote site.

Hardwired telemetry also matured during this period. Rather than concentrating on improving the reliability of the medium, the engineers who worked with wire telemetry devised and developed the concept of two-way communication, which allowed the train track switches not only to be monitored from a distance but also to be adjusted. Electric power utility companies and pipeline transportation companies had facilities that were comparable to those of the rail companies--large capital investments that required little in the way of complex control to operate. However, the switches and valves that had to be controlled were located at distant, inconvenient spots. Oil and gas production companies seemed to find most of their prizes in very inhospitable, poorly developed parts of the country where it was difficult to get operating crews to live. All of these industries responded to the same problem with the same solution: they investigated ways of remotely monitoring and controlling simple functions by using wire and electric signals to reduce the operating costs of their facilities. By the beginning of the 1960s, remote monitoring and supervisory control of several industrial processes was a developing technology.

Scientists and engineers recognized the improvements being made in radio technology for telemetry and applied them to this new two-way remote operation. Radio had transformed the gathering of weather information from a two-dimensional to a three-dimensional science. When radio was applied to the remote monitoring and control of processes, it changed this technology from one dimension, that is, along a railroad, pipeline, or electric transmission line, to two dimensions. Radio could be located almost anywhere on the surface of the Earth that it was needed.

Often, a combination of wire and radio was the most effective method for gathering and distributing signals. As radio improved, the costs of installation dropped, and more facilities could pass the economic feasibility hurdle. Installing buried telephone cable in remote areas can be extremely expensive. Radio paths are relatively immune to the condition of the intervening countryside as long as a line of sight exists between the transmitter and the receiver. During the 1960s, radio was used more and more. By the mid-1970s, radio became the communications path of choice for most newly installed two-way telemetry systems to fixed location facilities.

At the same time that radio was moving into the ascendancy, another electronic technology was developing. Digital computers made their debut in remote monitoring and supervisory control systems in the early 1960s. The increased flexibility they offered was very attractive to the designers of these systems. Early on, noncomputer systems had central stations that had grown in complexity; they required up to several thousand relays. Before the advent of electronic computers, in some cases these central stations had punched paper-tape programming. So-called mid-sized computers became available about 1965, and the stage was set for an explosion of systems that would allow massive centralizing of control. Large-scale communications, which often required leased long distance telephone lines in combination with privately owned radio systems, provided the paths to a very large number of field facilities. Often, the entire complement of a company's field facilities would be tied into one computer that was located hundreds of miles from the operation.

It was at the beginning of the 1970s that the term *SCADA* was coined and the word *telemetry* became began to fall out of use in describing two-way systems. Radio became so much better during the 1970s that it often replaced existing buried cable systems. Ground-dwelling rodents and backhoes couldn't do as much damage to radio signals as they could to buried cable. The stability of radio's frequency control also increased, requiring less maintenance. The reduced complexity of the equipment and the improved industrial design of the radio packaging made it possible to service the equipment in the field with less qualified technicians and less complicated service equipment.

The SCADA technology matured slowly during the late 1970s. Improvements in software resulted in better human-machine interfaces. Report writers were developed to provide the information that was wanted when it was wanted. Systems got bigger. As was the case with most industrial technologies, the development of powerful minicomputers had a profound effect on the development of SCADA. For one thing, smaller facilities could now be considered for remote operation. Perhaps the most profound effect, however, was that the minicomputer, which is usually the basis for the host computer or master terminal unit (MTU), became so inexpensive that it was no longer necessary to centralize the system. Of course, centralization could still be done where it made operational sense; but now, operational effectiveness rather than hardware cost could determine where the MTU was located. Industries such as electric utilities and pipelines retained their centralized philosophy; oil and gas production companies shifted to a more decentralized mode to put the control of the fields back in the hands of field operations specialists.

As systems proliferated, the radio spectrum became more fully utilized, and frequencies became harder and harder to get. As this was happening, other methods of radio communication were being developed, including satellite communications and cellular telephone. The costs for these communications methods dropped to the point where, with a few modifications to the SCADA system, they became the technology of choice in many systems.

This is where SCADA is today. It is expected that computer and communications improvements will continue to influence the development of the technology. Local area networks (LANs), which are dedicated, high-speed methods for communicating between digital hardware, are the hot communications subject now. Unit 14 will discuss the future of SCADA as it relates to LANs.

Exercises:

3-1. *By what decade had two-way remote control and monitoring become a recognized technology?*

3-2. *Name three factors that caused radio to be preferred over land lines for two-way remote control and monitoring.*

3-3. *Flexibility and the ease with which existing systems can be modified are two reasons that electronic computers supplemented built-for-purpose central controllers. What is another reason?*

3-4. *What was the most profound effect of the development of small, inexpensive minicomputers?*

3-5. *What factor do pipelines and electric transmission systems have in common with railroads that drove them to be early users of remote monitoring and control?*

Unit 4:
Real-Time Systems

UNIT 4

Real-Time Systems

For a long time, SCADA operated independently of other computer-based systems, and the issue of whether it was a real-time system was unimportant. Increasingly, however, we are now finding that SCADA is interfacing with applications that can operate on either a scheduled or a requested basis. A little thought about what SCADA systems are expected to do and, for that matter, what the letters in SCADA actually stand for will lead to the conclusion that SCADA fits somewhere between real-time and batch operation. It has elements of each. This unit will consider the aspects of SCADA systems that make them similar to real-time systems and how those aspects contribute to decisions affecting the design of SCADA systems.

Learning Objectives — When you have completed this unit, you should:

A. Understand the terms that deal with time response.

B. Understand the criteria to be considered when selecting scan interval.

C. Know the factors that affect decisions about where to place calculation or computing elements.

4-1. What Really Is Real Time?

The term *real-time control* is defined as "pertaining to the performance of a computation during the actual time that the related physical process transpires." In the context of SCADA it refers to the response of the control system to changes in the process. In rigorous terms, a real-time control system is one that introduces no time delay or dead time between the reception of a process measurement and the outputting of a control signal. In fact, nearly all control systems must introduce some time delay. Those that introduce an amount without any measurable effect are usually called real-time control systems. It may be helpful to think of batch mode control as being the opposite of real-time control.

Most systems that control continuous processes operate in real time. Consider Figure 4-1. The controlled variable signal is fed to the input of the control system with no time delay. The controller operates on this signal as quickly as possible with the control algorithm. The manipulated variable is output to the process immediately. Time delays exist in the control side of the system, but they are usually kept very short.

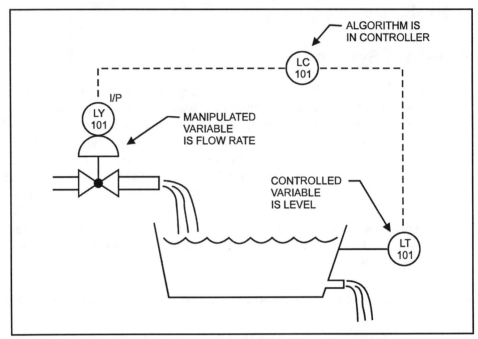

Figure 4-1. Most Continuous Process Control Minimizes Time Delay

Figure 4-2 shows a simple SCADA with the MTU scanning three RTUs. The MTU asks RTU number 1 for flow information about the flow through FE-101, then it asks each of the other RTUs about flow through their flow transmitters. The scan interval (sometimes called "scan period") is the time between one conversation with an RTU and the next conversation with the same RTU. It is obvious that the constraints of the SCADA system and its method of low-speed scanning are going to introduce a time delay.

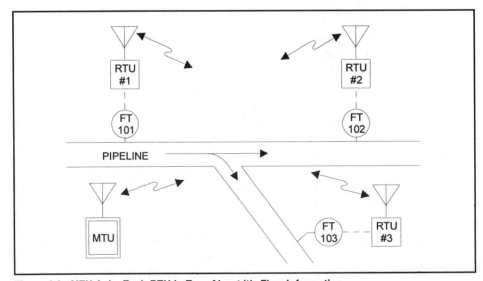

Figure 4-2. MTU Asks Each RTU In Turn About It's Flow Information

Figure 4-3 plots the delay. The decision whether to allow the control to be affected by the scan interval can only be made by someone familiar with the process. At the early stages of design of the SCADA system, scan interval can be selected to mitigate against some of the time delay effects. Section 4-3 will examine the process of tailoring the scan interval to the needs of the process.

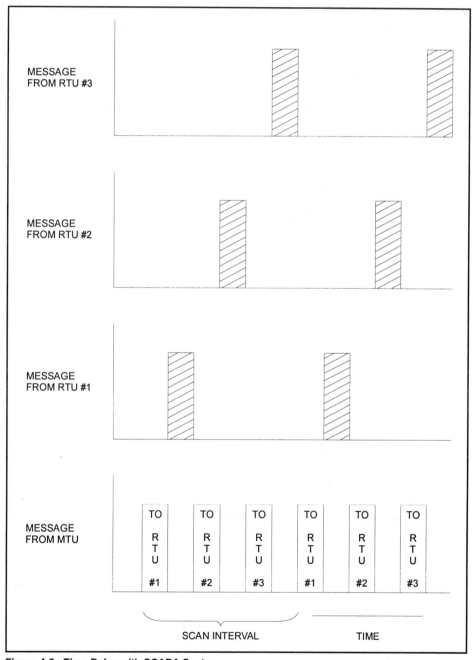

Figure 4-3. Time Delay with SCADA System

In particular, systems for indicating status or for alerting operators to process conditions that are out of limits (alarms) attempt to introduce as little time delay as "economically feasible." This is an important phrase when considering SCADA. It does not mean "as little time as possible." It means that the time response to the alarm must be considered when determining how quickly the alarm must be made known to the operator. The following three examples will help to clarify this. For each example, a process upset or equipment failure has been recognized. The SCADA system signals the operator that an alarm condition exists. The operator then responds to return the process to nominal.

Example 4-1. Out-of-limits condition: A beam pump on an oil well located at site 10-22 has stopped. Such pumps lift oil from the underground reservoir. When the pump stops, the flow of oil stops.

Alarm signal: "Beam pump 10-22 stopped."

Likely response: On the next scheduled visit to this part of the oil field, the field operator will plan to spend enough time at this site to determine the cause of the pump's failure, will write up a description of the failure, and will call in appropriate maintenance personnel to repair it.

The economically feasible time delay for this response is on the order of hours—perhaps as much as twenty-four hours.

Example 4-2. Out-of-limits condition: An electric submersible pump on an oil well located at site 6-33 has stopped.

Alarm signal: "Pump 6-33 stopped."

Likely response: Electric submersible pumps are expensive, high-volume pumps. For this reason, they are installed on high-volume wells. Because this well produces a very large amount of oil and downtime is important to the company, a maintenance crew will be dispatched, day or night, as soon as the alarm is received.

The economically feasible time delay for this response is on the order of minutes—perhaps as much as one hour.

Example 4-3. Out-of-limits condition: An electric switch between generator number G510 and the electric transmission system has opened.

Alarm signal: "Generator G510 switch open."

Likely response: A generator that is presently in the spinning reserve mode will be connected to the transmission grid as soon as possible.

The economically feasible time delay for this response is on the order of a few seconds—perhaps five seconds.

From these three examples, it should be clear that the response time the process requires should be the overriding consideration when determining what is and what is not "real time." Rigorously speaking, real time is response with no measurable time delay. Practically, real time means that the time delay of the system is not long enough to introduce problems in control. For this reason, much of SCADA is considered to be real-time control, even though a recognized time delay is associated with it.

4-2. Communications Access and "Master-Slave"

Electronic machines can talk to each other in several ways. Depending on the purpose of their conversation, the required speed, and the machines' status relative to each other, different access methods may be used. The communications requirements both determine and are controlled by the communications protocol selected.

This is not a text on communications, so it will not describe many of the communications access methods that exist. The communications method used by most existing SCADA systems is called "master-slave." In a master-slave arrangement, only one of the machines (in this case the host or MTU) is capable of initiating communication. The MTU calls one RTU, gives instructions, asks for information updates, and orders the RTU to respond. The MTU then listens for the answer. The RTU answers as soon as the MTU has finished talking, then stops talking and listens for more orders. The MTU moves to the second RTU and goes through the same procedure. The MTU talks to each RTU, then returns to the first. The RTU cannot initiate a message; it can send a message only when specifically ordered by the MTU to do so.

The process of talking to each RTU in order and then going back to the first RTU to begin the cycle all over again is called "scanning."

4-3. Determining Scan Interval

Control should not be compromised by excessive time delay; at the same time there are time constraints imposed by the rate at which data can be transferred to and from the RTU. It therefore follows that there is a "best rate" at which to scan the RTUs for data. One of the factors that determines scan interval must be the number of RTUs that have to be scanned. An estimate of the likely number of RTUs, made early in the design phase, will probably be sufficient to determine what this number is.

A second factor to be considered is the amount of data that must be passed on each conversation. This will be determined by the size of the facility at each remote site and the amount of independence the remote site control is capable of exercising. Depending on these, the data to be gathered can be as little as one status point or as much as several hundred status and alarm points, as well as several dozen meter totalizer points and several dozen analog values. To communicate, each status or alarm point requires one (usually) or two bits (less frequently) of data. Since each meter or analog point will be transcribed to a binary word, each point requires about sixteen bits. (This will vary with different equipment but is a close enough number for this calculation.)

For simplicity as well as for safety reasons, it is best to select the largest RTU when evaluating points. Multiply this point count by the total number of RTUs to get the count of all data coming back from all RTUs. Remember that a conversation is usually a transfer of data in both directions. It is important to include the time taken for the MTU to talk to each RTU. This will include both the time for the MTU to ask the RTU for information and the time for the MTU to give other instructions to each RTU. Again, at the design stage the best way to take these two times into account is to evaluate what this point count is for the largest outgoing message and then multiply by the number of RTUs. This should provide a conservative result because the messages from MTU to RTU are usually shorter than the messages from RTU to MTU. Evaluating each RTU individually may be beneficial if the exercise is being done on an existing system.

The third factor is the data rate. The number of bits per second (bps) that can be transmitted over the communications medium is important in determining scan interval, but at the early design stages this number may be flexible. Bps numbers may be traded back and forth to develop an optimum. At this point in the process of determining scan interval, consider that there are two data rate groupings. The first, which is used on voice-grade telephone lines and most UHF radio-modem communications systems, is between 300 and 2400 bps. Using 1200 bps in the calculation will give you a good first estimate. The second data rate grouping applies if a special communications medium is being considered. It may be as low as 19,200 bps or as high as 10 million bps. For systems that are complex enough to require these data rates there will be a specialist on the design team who can provide a meaningful data rate for this calculation.

The fourth factor in determining scan interval is communications efficiency, which may be thought of through the following ratio: the time spent moving the data of interest divided by the total time spent communicating. Much of the inefficiency is obvious. For example, part of each message must include the RTU address, which is not really data that holds any interest. Some of the inefficiency is not so obvious, however. Error-detection codes are frequently used, and these take time. Similarly, radio turn-on times may take more time than the message. These will be dealt with in Units 6 and 7, respectively, but as a first approximation use the following numbers for communications efficiency: dedicated telephone line, 70 percent; radio, 40 percent; dial-up telephone, less than 1 percent.

Example 4-4. Based on the preceding discussion, calculate a scan interval for a SCADA system.

1. It will initially have seven RTUs but will likely increase eventually to twenty. Therefore, the number of RTUs equals twenty.

2. The largest RTU has the following point counts:

140 status points	140
30 alarm points	30
10 measurement meters (at sixteen bits each)	160
10 analog points (at sixteen bits each)	160

    The MTU will send the following point counts to the RTU:

150 discrete control (valves, motors) points	150
6 stepping motor positions (at sixteen bits each)	96
10 valve controller set points (at sixteen bits each)	160
Total points	896

3. Data rate is based on the likelihood that UHF radio will be used for communication. Use 1200 bps.

4. Communications efficiency, based on UHF radio, is 40 percent.

Therefore, 20 × 896 = 20,000 bits to move at a data rate of 1200 bps, which would take 20,000 bits ÷ 1,200 bps = 17 seconds at 100 percent efficiency.

At 40 percent efficiency, the scan interval is 17 seconds ÷ 0.4 = 42.5 seconds. It would be good design practice to round this 42 seconds up to one minute. Having calculated this number, it would be wise to ensure that no process functions will be adversely affected by a delay of one minute. If such functions do exist but only at one or two of the RTUs, the problems may be addressed by scanning each of those RTUs twice in the scan.

Example 4-5. If the scan rate were acceptable for all except RTU number 5 in a system of five RTUs, the scanning program could be set up as follows:

RTU 1, RTU 2, RTU 5, RTU 3, RTU 4, RTU 5, RTU 1...

As with most quick-fix solutions, there are limits to how often this can be done without degrading the rest of the system.

If most of the RTUs show process functions that are marginally good or bad from a timing point of view, the best solution may be to increase the data rate (in this case, from 1200 bps to 2400 bps). It is important to realize that doubling the data rate will not reduce the scan period by one half. Communications efficiency is a nonlinear function of data rate. If many problems are identified and the process requires a response time that is orders-of-magnitude shorter than the problems will allow, it may be necessary to review the communications method. It may be that some functions should be removed from the SCADA system.

Provision should be made for additions to the amount of data to be transmitted. Most SCADA systems have functions added to them over their lives; few have functions deleted. Unit 5 will address some of the activities that should not be dependent on the communications system. The next section of this unit will discuss options for locating computing or calculating elements.

4-4.   Where to Compute?

Have you noticed as you travel on a freeway that is well lighted by mercury or sodium lamps that the spokes on the hubcaps of the car next to you are visible and are slowly turning—sometimes backward, sometimes forward? This is the "strobe effect," and it happens because the street lights give off a burst of light every 1/60 second (every 1/50 second if your power system is 50 Hz). If the spokes of the hubcap are turning so that a spoke is at (or near) the same position that another spoke was 1/60th of a second ago, your eyes will be fooled into thinking they are seeing the same spoke.

Figure 4-4 shows how this works. To clarify the illustration, one of the spokes (the one in the twelve o'clock position) in Figure 4-4(A) has been smeared by road tar. If we assume a 30-inch-diameter wheel with six spokes, the configuration shown in Figure 4-4(B) will happen 1/60 of a second later if the car is going 53.55 mph, and the configuration in Figure 4-4(C) will happen 1/60 second after that of Figure 4-4(B).

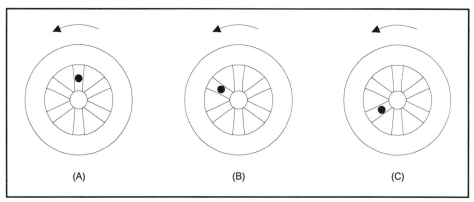

Figure 4-4. Sampling Frequency and "Aliasing"

Now take off the road tar. Imagine that the car is going 107.1 mph or 160.65 mph or any integral multiple of 53.55 mph. If you could see (or sample) only the relative position of the spokes, you would have no way to tell how fast the car is going. The spokes would not appear to move. If the car were going a bit slower, the hubcap would appear to rotate backward; if the car were moving a bit faster, it would appear to rotate forward slowly.

So, for a case that has the physical constraints we have described, there is something magic about 53.55 mph and the sampling frequency of 60 Hz. The "magic" is that for every integral multiple of 53.55 mph, a spoke (we don't know which one) passes through the top vertical position. Now turn the problem around. Say we know that the range of speeds is between 0 mph and 53.55 mph and we wish to calculate the minimum frequency of the strobe so we can unambiguously determine the speed. How could we do it?

Since we know that it takes 1/60 of a second for the spoke to advance one position, we must fire the strobe a bit faster than 1/60 of a second if we want to sample the situation that exists before the spoke gets there. The frequency must be faster than 60 Hz, because at 60 Hz one spoke could masquerade as another. In this example, 60 Hz is called the "aliasing frequency." For a similar situation in which the number of spokes is changed to twelve, the aliasing frequency would be 120 Hz.

This is all very interesting, you say, but what does it have to do with SCADA? If the physical attributes of the process to be controlled, including the highest natural frequency of the process, are known the aliasing frequency can be calculated. The process parameters can be sampled effectively at frequencies higher than the aliasing frequency but not at lower frequencies. So this simple test of how frequently the process must be sampled can tell if the scan frequency is adequate for sampling. If it is adequate and if the measurement is not too critical, the process can be sampled, the raw data can be scanned, the calculation (or computation) can be done in the MTU, and the result can be sent back to the RTU and processed. On the other hand, those processes that have aliasing frequencies higher than the selected scanning frequency must have the computations done before the scanning. These computations must take place in the RTU or some other equipment at the same location as the RTU. The following two examples will illustrate this point.

Example 4-6. Given that, from Example 4-4, a scan interval of one minute is practical, determine where the calculations should be performed to measure the amount of water produced from a well using a tank metering system. Such metering systems are used on irrigated farms to keep track of the amount of water diverted to a field. Water flows into the tank until it is full, then stops. A valve is then opened to start the flow of water from the tank to the field. When the tank becomes empty, the drain valve closes, and the tank refills. It takes four minutes to fill the tank and four minutes to drain the tank. Status switches on the drain valve are monitored by the SCADA system. When the drain valve is closed, the refill valve is open and vice versa.

Question: Can the flow totalizing be done at the MTU?

Answer: Since the scan interval is one minute (from Example 4-1) and the aliasing frequency (the highest cycling frequency in the process) is one cycle (of the refill valve) in four minutes, this calculation would be an acceptable one to do at the MTU.

Example 4-7. Question: Assume the same conditions as in Example 4-6, except that only forty seconds are required to refill the tank. Can the flow totalizing be done at the RTU?

Answer: Since the drain valve contains operating frequencies (one cycle ÷ 40 seconds or 0.025 Hz) higher than the scan frequency (one cycle ÷ 60 seconds or 0.017 Hz), there will be cycles that are short enough for the valve to close and then open before the SCADA system completes a scan. The MTU will have no way to know that the cycle happened. In this case, the totalizing should be done at the RTU. Note that the entire operation may cycle in less than a scan period, but if the part of the cycle that is being sampled cycles in less than a scan period you will get the wrong measurement. The RTU should use a sampling frequency higher than the MTU scan frequency and one designed to cover the process aliasing frequency. But as we will see in Unit 8, that is not an onerous requirement. The periods of scan intervals within most RTUs are usually on the order of milliseconds.

Given that some rather simple calculations can be used to determine which computations should be done at the MTU and which should be done at the RTU, there remains the question of what hardware should be used to perform auxiliary calculations at the RTU's location. Because of the enormous reduction in the cost of small computer hardware, it is now feasible to purchase a computer that is powerful enough to complete, in a timely manner, all of the calculations, all of the instruction to sensors, and all of the storage of historical data that may be needed at the site. This means that it is possible to have the computer-based RTU do all of the remote site calculations.

The reasons why you do not want to put "all your eggs in one basket" are several. As will be explained in Unit 10, safety-related control considerations call for the use of fail-safe logic for safety shutdowns. Regulatory requirements may mandate that meter totalizer logic be located in separate locked enclosures. Small, simple RTUs supported by special-purpose logic modules may be more price competitive than large, complex RTUs that require no support. Finally, some control calculations require input data from more than one remote site. These control functions are most logically completed at the MTU. Simple orders can be sent to the appropriate RTUs to effect these controls.

EXERCISES

4-1. *Real time is relative. For the following process concerns, determine if the response time is adequate:*

    a.   *Customer billing for gas through a meter is issued once per month. The scan rate is once per hour.*

    b.   *Customer billing for gasoline is based on individual fill-ups, each lasting ninety seconds. The scan rate of the meter is once per hour.*

    c.   *Two meters measuring gas into and out of a pipeline are scanned every ten minutes. An alarm is generated if the sum of the last four inlet measurements exceeds the sum of the last four outlet measurements.*

4-2. *An RTU recognizes that a motor that should be running has stopped. It is 2:00 a.m. For this motor failure, overtime is not allowed, so no maintenance crew will be sent to investigate until 9:00 a.m.*

    a.   *Would a ten-minute scan rate be acceptable?*
    b.   *Would a one-hour scan rate be acceptable?*
    c.   *Would a twenty-four-hour scan rate be acceptable?*

4-3. *An RTU determines that a fire is burning in the chlorine injection building of a water treatment plant. Because this is an extremely serious condition, what can the RTU do to notify the MTU without waiting for the next scan?*

4-4. Describe one way that the scan rate for a single RTU could be increased beyond the scan rate for the other RTUs.

4-5. What is the range of data rates for most SCADA systems?

4-6. Name three things that detract from communications efficiency.

4-7. In Example 4-1, what would be the scan interval if a dedicated telephone line, not a UHF radio, were the communications medium?

4-8. The liquid level in a column gravity separator is observed to cycle with a two-minute period from one maximum level to the next. What would be the effect of sampling this level with the following:

a. A two-minute scan rate?
b. A thirty-second scan rate?

Unit 5:
Remote Control —
What Not to SCADA

UNIT 5

Remote Control — What Not to SCADA

Every technology has applications for which it seems admirably suited, other applications for which it seems only marginally suited, and a group of applications for which it simply should not be used. When a technology is very young, it is often not clear which of those applications should be avoided. As the technology matures, the hard school of experience clarifies some of them. In this unit, we will discuss whether some types of control and data acquisition applications should depend on SCADA for their operation.

Learning Objectives — When you have completed this unit, you should:

A. Recognize that some process control and data acquisition functionality should not be handled remotely.

B. Anticipate the type and magnitude of problems that can and will assail a SCADA system.

C. Be able to develop solutions to the potential problems that will hamper a SCADA system.

5-1. Murphy's Law and Remote Control

Murphy lives! If you want to prove it, butter a slice of bread and drop it on the floor. If your intention is to prove that it will always fall butter-side down, you will almost certainly note that this is so only about 50 percent of the time. On the other hand, if you drop it accidentally it always falls butter-side down. In a similar way, a remote control system or a data acquisition system can be counted on to perform flawlessly until that moment when a message absolutely must be sent or a piece of data essential to the financial continuity of the company is working its way from one end of the system to the other. Then it will fail.

You can test it. You can perform all manner of evaluations on each and every individual part of the system. You can run performance checks on the system as a whole. You can consult the experts. How many times has this author been told by maintenance technical specialists, "That system must be absolutely reliable. It hasn't failed since I've been here!" Believe it: If you depend on a remote control system to handle some critical function, it will fail. The more critical the function is, the faster and more catastrophically it will fail.

Over the years, signals that could potentially be placed on a SCADA system have been evaluated to determine which ones could cause a problem. The specific signals that individual industries need will vary, but the general types of signals are fairly constant. Two types should not be designed to depend on SCADA: the first are safety instrumented systems and the second are product measurement systems that will be used for billing or paying taxes and thus will require audit trails.

5-2. Safety Instrumented Systems

All processes should be equipped with a safety instrumented system if through the failure of some part they may cause injury to a member of the public or a worker or may cause damage to the equipment or the environment. Safety instrumented systems should be designed to override the normal control systems. They may be manually or automatically initiated.

The normal control system, of course, is designed to monitor the operating parameters of the process and to make adjustments as necessary to keep the process within limits. This will assure that the product meets predefined specifications and that process and related equipment do not leak, burn, explode, or otherwise come into potentially harmful contact with bystanders. But the normal control system does not always work properly. Sometimes this is a result of mechanical failure. Sometimes the feedstock didn't meet specs or the energy source failed. Occasionally, the targets that the operator established for the normal controls to achieve were incorrect. Figure 5-1 lists the three characteristics around which safety instrumented systems are designed.

| 1.   SHOULD BE ABLE TO OVERRIDE NORMAL CONTROL SYSTEM. |
| 2.   SHOULD NOT SHARE COMPONENTS WITH NORMAL CONTROLS. |
| 3.   SHOULD BE AS SIMPLE AS POSSIBLE. |

Figure 5-1. Three Main Design Characteristics of Safety Instrumented Systems

If the safety instrumented system is designed to override the normal control system it may operate to keep the process safe even when several failures occur simultaneously in the control system. If the safety instrumented system is designed so that its integrity does not depend on the continued operation of those elements of the normal control system, the joint reliability of the two systems will be improved. And, if the safety instrumented system follows the maxim of the U.S. Army, "KISS" (Keep It Simple, Stupid!), with a minimum number of parts, electrical contacts, and instructions, it will invariably work better.

The last two of these three conditions of safety instrumented systems argue against the inclusion of the SCADA system in the safety instrumented system. With respect to the continued operation of the control system, it would be feasible to tie the sensors and actuators dedicated to the safety instrumented system into the SCADA. It would usually not be feasible to install a second RTU, communications system, or MTU just for the safety instrumented system. Figure 5-2 shows how complex the situation could get for even a simple system.

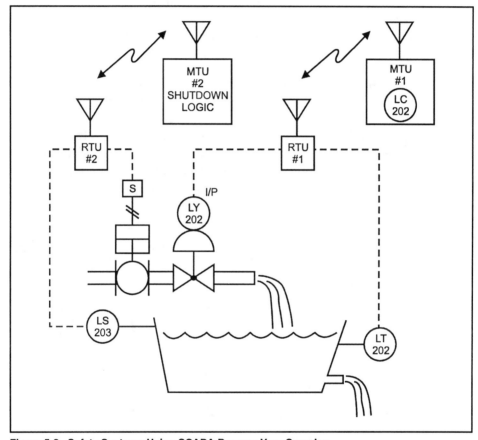

Figure 5-2. Safety Systems Using SCADA Become Very Complex

"Keeping it simple" may be a relative concept, but few qualified designers would argue that SCADA is sufficiently simple to qualify as an appropriate element for a safety instrumented system. This is not to say that SCADA cannot be used to enhance the safety of geographically diverse systems. Pipelines are often protected from leaks by measuring inflow and outflow, subtracting the two, and closing block valves along the line if the difference gets too large. What it does say, however, is that the sensing, logic, and actuation features of a safety instrumented system at a local site should not rely on the SCADA system. In fact, the design of a process that is to be controlled and monitored by a SCADA system should always include an assessment of the result of each conceivable type of failure of the SCADA. These assessments will identify some failures that can be classed as "high risk."

Risk is measured as the product of probability and consequence. If the probability is high and the consequence is negligible, then the risk is not high. Similarly, if the probability approaches zero but the consequence is high, then the risk is not high. But in some conditions the probability of failure will be reasonably high and the consequences of failure will be serious; such conditions will indicate a high-risk situation. Figure 5-3 shows a matrix of this method for establishing generic risk.

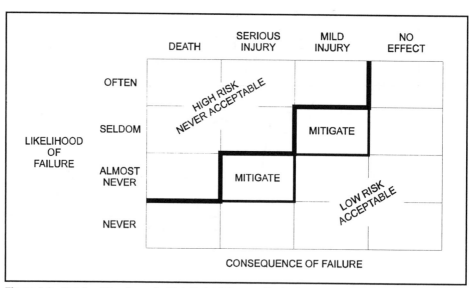

Figure 5-3. Matrix of the Generic Risk Establishment Method

The evaluation of risk is becoming an engineering specialty in its own right. It should be undertaken by people who are familiar with the process, equipment, operating conditions, and evaluation methods. High-risk failures should be guarded against by installing local safety instrumented systems. ISA has developed a standard, SP84

"Programmable Electronic Systems for use in Safety Systems," that deals with the requirements of safety instrumented systems.

Figure 5-4 shows an example of a SCADA-operated valve with a local loop override. In this case, high liquid level will cause the valve to close even if the SCADA system tries to open it. Example 5-1 illustrates one of the few high-risk applications in which SCADA is involved in safety instrumented systems. Even here local loop protection may be provided.

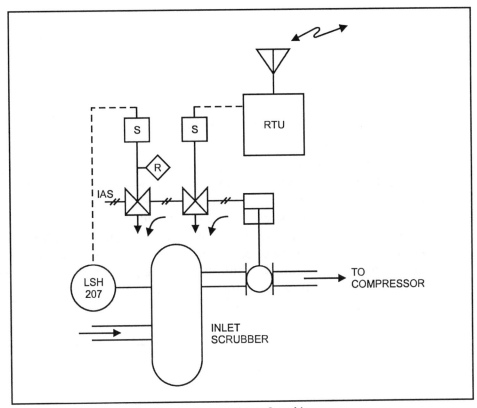

Figure 5-4. SCADA-operated Valve with Local Loop Override

Example 5-1. A SCADA system monitors the inflow and outflow of a liquid hydrocarbon pipeline. Refer to Figure 5-5. At the MTU location, calculations are done to determine if the inflow is equal to or less than the outflow. If more liquid is measured going into the line than going out of it, the MTU will recognize a leak and will send a message to the RTU at each end that will cause a block valve at each of those two locations to close. As an alternative, the MTU may send an alarm message to the operator who will then decide whether to block in the line with the remote-operated valves.

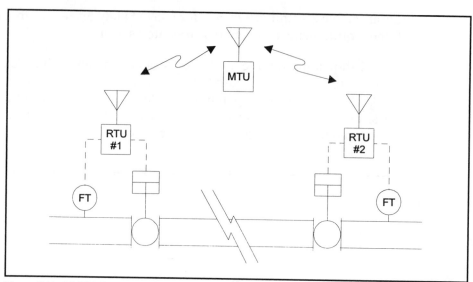

Figure 5-5. SCADA System in Liquid Hydrocarbon Pipeline

Murphy has the power to cause the radio at either one of the RTU sites or the MTU site (or all three for that matter) to become unserviceable at just that time. Rather than allow the pump to continue forcing oil into the line, the designer should assume that the MTU will not send a timely shutdown instruction. A local shutdown loop, as shown in Figure 5-6, that is based on low pressure or on the rate of change of pressure drop will not detect small leaks as quickly but will provide protection for large leaks. The large ones are those with the most severe consequences.

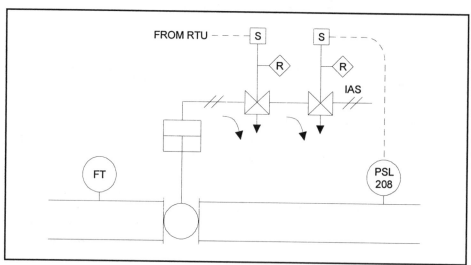

Figure 5-6. Local Shutdown Loop

5-3.   Regulatory Requirements

The computer is bringing on the age of the paperless society. That may be difficult to believe for anyone who is on forty mailing lists for computer-generated junk mail or who stores all of his or her e-mail on paper printouts. But even if we are approaching such a paperless society, some authorities insist that certain data have a "paper trail." Some of these authorities have almost as much power as Murphy. They certainly have enough to make it worthwhile for system designers to listen. These authorities are the ones who are responsible for ensuring that the taxes, royalties, tariffs, and so on are paid in the correct amount.

Most industries follow government regulations requiring that something be measured and the measurement be reported to one or more government agencies. Often, the numbers reported represent large amounts of money that must be paid to the government. Examples of this process include the measurement of oil from a well, which requires that a royalty be paid, or the measurement of irrigation water from a government-owned reservoir, which requires that a fee be paid. Many industries have associates, customers, or suppliers that they exchange products with. The products may represent large cash values. If each of the parties is considered to be "sophisticated," rules will be established between the buyer and the seller to govern the method of measuring and billing for the product transfer. Examples of this include electric utilities sending blocks of electric power across their transmission line for a fee or a pipeline company moving batches of clean natural gas through a pipeline for a tariff.

Some industries supply thousands of relatively small amounts of product to the general public. In these cases, the monetary value of each transaction may be small, but there are large numbers of transactions. Governments recognize that the public is "unsophisticated" about measurement and accounting techniques. For this reason, they often put in regulations in place that require that these measurements and accounting procedures follow certain forms. Each of these types of transactions will be required by at least one party in order to establish a paper trail.

The term *paper trail* comes from the method auditors use to check that a true accounting has been made. They start with one piece of paper, such as a request for quotation. They then move to the next paper, which would be the quotations submitted, and on to the next papers, which may be the evaluation of the quotes, the order itself, the materials receipt, the invoice, the check, and then the final receipt. In following this trail, they can determine whether or not the proper procedures were followed, whether the right amount of material was delivered, whether the right amount of money was paid, and whether the proper people received the money.

This accounting procedure has proved to work well. It is not going to be supplanted by another method just because SCADA systems are capable of electronically moving some of those data elements that were once moved in triplicate on variously colored pieces of paper. In fact, compromises are currently being reached to allow more than paper records to form part of the paper trail. Many of these compromises recognize that electronic data is more ephemeral than paper, and they therefore require that a considerable amount of time must pass before this data can be erased from the primary measurement device, even after it has been transmitted to the data collection device. Some of the compromises are more along the lines of the belt-and-suspenders combination, requiring that a physical printout be made on a daily basis even though the billing numbers are sent electronically.

Allowance may also be made for the fact that computer programs designed to calculate volumes or amounts of energy can be changed more easily than the mechanical devices that used to be used to make the measurements. The security procedures for the devices on which these computer programs reside may be extensive, even including housing them in locked metal boxes. However, the more likely approach, the controlled access of passwords, is acceptable.

The paper trail will probably not have to be fashioned out of paper, but some method for making an audit is required. Almost certainly, the primary measurement calculation should be done at the RTU location. It should also be stored at that location for some time afterward, perhaps as long as thirty-five days. Figure 5-7 shows a typical printout for a primary measurement calculation.

The regulations that deal with these measurements vary from jurisdiction to jurisdiction and also from industry to industry. You should be aware that such regulations are likely wherever the custody of a material is transferred. You certainly should plan to acquire the data on your SCADA system, but you should also plan to acquire backup data by other means.

NOMINAL OIL AND GAS CO. LTD.

GAS METERING STATION NO 1009
METER POINT NO 1009

DATE OF PRINTOUT 961020

STANDARD FACTORS
—PIPE DIAM.   201.3 mm
—ORIFICE SIZE   100.0 mm
—BASE PRESS.   101.325 kPag
—BASE TEMP.   15.0 °C

DATE YY/MM/DD	TIME HH/MM	DAY RATE km^3/D	CUM TOTAL kM^3
96/10/19	23/59	121.62	2431.09
96/10/18	23/58	122.47	2309.47
96/10/18	00/01	121.22	2187.00
96/10/16	23/59	120.14	2065.78
96/10/15	23/59	112.09	1945.64
96/10/14	23/58	109.11	1833.55
96/10/13	23/59	118.77	1724.44

Figure 5-7. Typical Printout for a Primary Measurement Calculation

Exercises:

5-1.   Safety instrumented systems override control systems, are independent of control systems in terms of their elements, and are designed to have few parts. Which two of these three characteristics indicate that SCADA should not be used for safety instrumented systems?

5-2.   The level of liquid in a tank is measured by a displacer that outputs a signal to a valve controller. When the level gets above a preselected amount, the controller causes the valve to pinch back, reducing flow into the tank. Can a signal from this displacer be monitored by the SCADA system?

5-3.   Should a signal from the displacer in Exercise 5-2 be used for a protective override of the valve actuator?

5-4.   What is there about communications systems that suggests they should not be used for safety instrumented systems?

5-5.   Electric transmission systems are often equipped with SCADA packages that can develop trends. From these trends, it is possible to predict when parts of the line will become overloaded. Should remote switches be installed to allow the operator to isolate these sections of line?

5-6.   *What other protection should be in place to protect these lines?*

5-7.   *In addition to safety instrumented systems, what other function should not be dependent on SCADA? Why not?*

5-8.   *Why do some regulatory bodies insist that the algorithm used to calculate fluid volumes be printed out by each flow totalizer once a day?*

Unit 6:
Communications

UNIT 6

Communications

Communications is the movement of data or intelligence from one location to another. For communications to happen, several things must be in place. First, a communications path must exist; some medium must be selected over which the data will travel. Second, equipment must exist at the sending end of the communications path to condition the data and to put it into a form that can be sent over the communications medium. Third, equipment must exist at the receiving end of the path to extract the message from the medium and understand its meaning.

This unit will discuss some of the communications equipment and media that can be used for SCADA as well as some of the factors to consider in selecting them. We will also introduce some of the concepts and terms used in communications.

Learning Objectives — When you have completed this unit, you should:

A. Know the functions, benefits, and shortcomings of common communications equipment used in SCADA systems.

B. Be able to understand the communications terms as they relate to remote data acquisition and control.

6-1. Communications Makes SCADA Possible

Given that a SCADA system consists of one or more MTUs sending instructions to and receiving data from one or more RTUs, it is clear that communications plays a vital role in the operation of the system.

Installing SCADA is usually justified because of the remoteness of a site and the difficulty or cost of manning it. In some few cases, it is dangerous, unhealthy, or otherwise unpleasant for a person to be at a site. In most cases, it is simply too expensive to have an operator stay at the site for extended periods of time or even to visit the site on a once-a-shift or once-a-day basis.

As long as some type of communications path can be established between the remote sites and the central or master site, data can be passed. If a communications link cannot be established, a SCADA system cannot be developed.

6-2.   Data Is Binary: Analog-to-Digital Conversion

All data moved between the MTU and the RTUs is binary data. It may have originated that way as a status condition of an on-off switch, or it may have been converted to binary form from analog form. Figure 6-1 shows the output from a limit switch that may be used to indicate the state of a valve. In Figure 6-1(a), the valve is open and the switch output is a steady +5 volts. In Figure 6-1(b), the valve is closed and the switch output is a steady 0 volts. Note that the switch output is 0 volts at any time that the valve is not completely open. This feature can be used to advantage. If you need to know when the valve is not closed, you can arrange to have it output 5 volts at all times except when it is completely closed. The bottom part of Figure 6-1(c) shows a switch output for a valve that is open, then closed, then open, and so on.

Figure 6-2 shows how the switch output from a valve is changed to a bit. The word *bit* stands for **binary digit**. A single-bit register, or flip-flop, is shown in Figure 6-2(a). The valve status switch output is fed to the enable input of the register, and the register binary output signal comes out of the register. A continuous series of pulses, called the clock, is fed into another

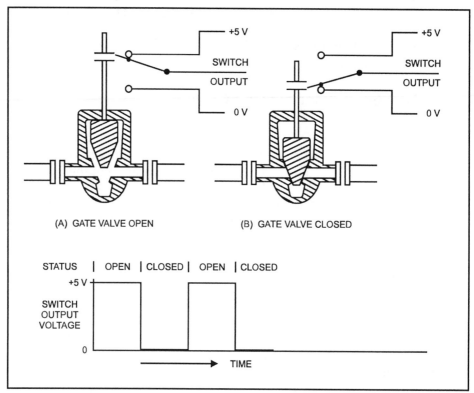

Figure 6-1. Output from a Limit Switch

input of the register. Figure 6-2(b) shows the timing of the logic. Shortly before time = 1, the valve opens, and the valve status switch output moves from 0 volts to +5 volts. At time = 1, the clock pulse goes positive (from 0 volts to +5 volts), and this, combined with +5 volts on the enable input of the register, causes the register to output a "1" (see the bottom line of Figure 6-2[b]).

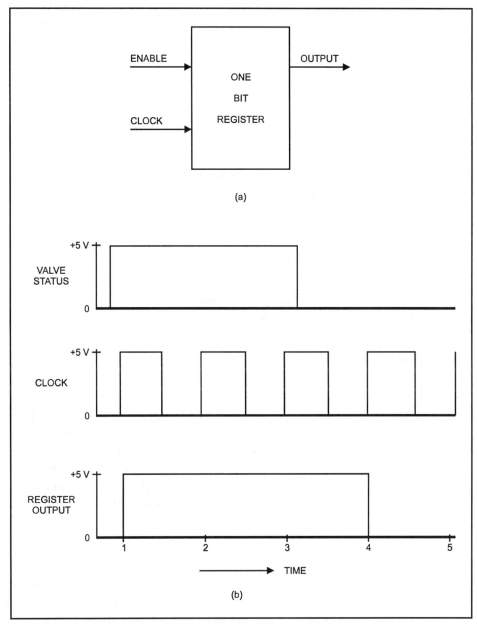

Figure 6-2. Valve Switch Output Changed to a Bit

The valve stays open for several clock periods and closes after time = 3. When it does, the enable signal goes to 0 volts, but this does not change the register output. When the clock pulse goes positive at time = 4, the register output changes to a "0." Additional detail will be provided about these signals in Unit 8. Figure 6-3 shows how an analog signal is developed to represent a valve position. When the valve stem rises to its fully open position, the transmitter output will be +5.000 volts. When the valve is fully closed, the output will be 0.000 volts. As shown in Figure 6-3, the output is at some value between 0 and 5 volts. Let us assume that it is +3.000 volts.

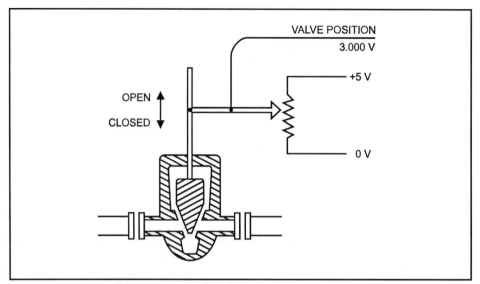

Figure 6-3. Analog Signal Developed to Represent a Valve Position

Instead of going directly to a register, the +3.000-volt analog signal is sent to an analog-to-digital converter (ADC), shown in Figure 6-4, that will change it to a series of binary digits and store these bits in a register. Usually, there are eight to sixteen bits in this kind of register, but for simplicity only four bits will be used in this example. The largest bit is usually called the most significant bit or MSB; the smallest is the least significant bit or LSB. The MSB is one half the value of the full-scale amount. Each succeeding bit is one half the value of the previous bit.

Starting at the top left of Figure 6-4, the 3.000-volt signal is fed to the first stage of the converter. The converter tries to subtract 2.500 volts from it. It can (because 3.000 is larger than 2.500), so it outputs a +5-volt signal to the enable input of the 2.500-volt bit (MSB) of the register. The next positive-going clock pulse will force the register MSB to output a "1." The remainder (3.000 - 2.500 = 0.500 volts) is fed to the second stage. The converter tries to subtract 1.250 volts from it. It cannot (because 0.500 is smaller than 1.250), so it outputs a 0-volt signal to the enable input of the 1.250-volt bit of the register. The next clock will force that register bit to a "0."

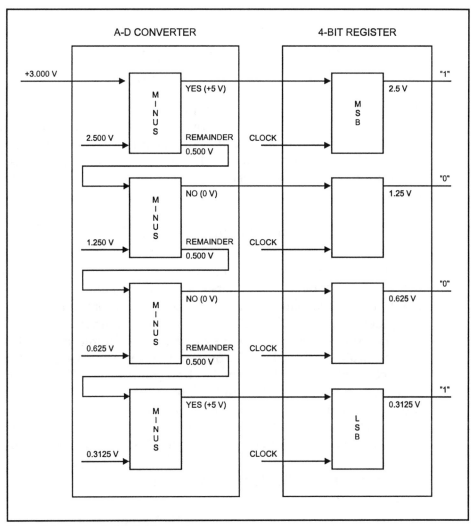

Figure 6-4. Analog-to-Digital Converter

The remainder (still 0.500 volts) is fed to the third stage. The converter tries to subtract 0.625 volts from it. It cannot (because 0.500 is smaller than 0.625) so it outputs a 0-volt signal to the enable input of the 0.625-volt bit of the register. The next clock will force that register bit to a "0." The remainder (still 0.500 volts) is fed to the fourth stage. The converter tries to subtract 0.3125 volts from it. It can, so it outputs a +5-volt signal to the enable input of the LSB of the register. The next clock bit will force that register bit to a "1."

The final result is a four-bit binary word that describes the 3.000 volts as follows:

$$
\begin{array}{lrcl}
\text{MSB} & 1 \times 2.500 \text{ volts} & = & 2.500 \text{ volts} \\
& +0 \times 1.250 \text{ volts} & = & 0 \text{ volts} \\
& +0 \times 0.625 \text{ volts} & = & 0 \text{ volts} \\
\text{LSB} & +1 \times 0.3125 \text{ volts} & = & \underline{.3125} \text{ volts} \\
& & & 2.8125 \text{ volts}
\end{array}
$$

Because a four-bit register provides precision of 1 in 2^4, or 1 in 16, of the full-scale value, this is as close as we can get to 3.000 volts. For some applications, the signal will vary from positive to negative, using up one additional bit. Additional bits would provide additional precision. Accuracy is sometimes defined in terms of plus or minus one half of the least significant bit (LSB).

6-3.   Long Distance Communications Is Serial

All data moved between the MTU and the RTUs is serial. That means that a single string of binary characters is sent one after another. The alternative to serial is parallel. Parallel buses are used within computers and from computers to printers, but the cost of the extra communications medium (wire) becomes prohibitive for long distance communications paths. To communicate the digital word from the ADC in Section 6-2 in serial format, some convention must be defined to transmit first the MSB, then the next smaller, then the next smaller until all bits are sent. Or some convention must be defined to transmit first the LSB followed by the next larger, followed by the next larger, and so on. This convention would be part of the communications protocol, which will be discussed in Section 6-5.

6-4.   Communications System Components

Figure 6-5 illustrates a very simple SCADA system that consists of one MTU and one RTU. Somehow the MTU and the RTU must be equipped to communicate with each other. In telecommunications parlance, the MTU and the RTU are each called "data terminal equipments" (DTEs). They each have the ability to formulate a signal that contains the intelligence that must be sent. They also each have the ability to decipher a received signal to extract its intelligence. What they lack is the capacity to interface with the medium.

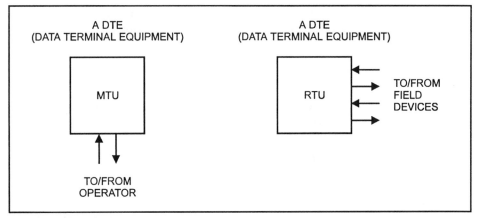

Figure 6-5. Very Simple SCADA System

Figure 6-6 interposes equipment that has that capacity to interface. The modems, which can be called "data communication equipments" (DCEs), are able to receive information from the DTEs, make necessary changes to the form of the information, and send it out over the medium to other DCEs, which will receive it and transform it before passing it to a DTE. More information about modems will be presented in Section 6-6.

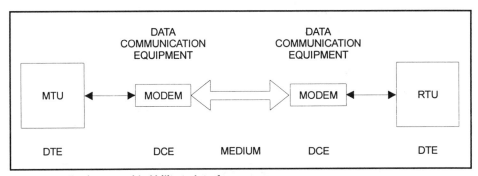

Figure 6-6. Equipment with Ability to Interface

The International Organization for Standardization (ISO) has developed the Open Systems Interconnection (OSI) model (see Figure 6-7). It consists of seven layers. The OSI model defines the function of each layer, and the intent is that when the appropriate number of layers is supplied for any two machines communication between them will be possible.

The upper layer and the lower two layers, that is, layers seven, two, and one, are sufficient for most SCADA communications systems. It is important to note that there is not necessarily a direct correspondence between an OSI layer, which defines a function, and a physical piece of hardware. Most of the functionality of layer one and some of the functionality of level two can be thought of as occurring in the modem. Some of the functionality of layer two can be thought of as occurring in the MTU or the RTU.

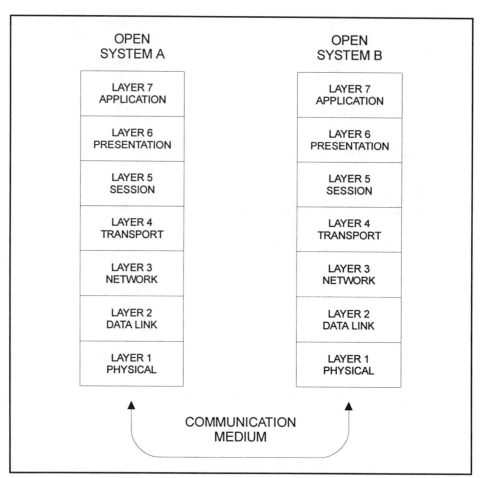

Figure 6-7. Open Systems Interconnection (OSI) Model

6-5.   Protocol

Protocol will be discussed in much detail in Unit 8. For now it is important to know that a protocol is a set of rules that defines the meaning of a pattern of binary words. It has been established that the messages to be sent from the MTU to the RTU are a series of binary digits. But what will the first bit represent? the second? the 247th? Protocol tells us. It supplies the code to create this long series of ones and zeros. The same code allows the receiving station to decode it.

The same code used by the sender must be used by the receiver. This is not to say that only one protocol is available; there are dozens. Equipment manufacturers developed them before any standards organizations became interested. Many equipment manufacturers continued to use their proprietary protocols even after the standards organizations had developed open standards, and some even developed new proprietary standards after these open standards were available. Some are better for certain applications than others. Some are worse for all applications than others. The important thing to know about them is that one absolutely must have the same protocol at the RTU as at the MTU.

Figure 6-8 shows the layout of a message sent in a particular protocol based on IEEE C37.1. The purpose of each bit is defined. The total length of the transmitted document is included as the sum of all fixed bits plus the number of bits carried in the "data" frame. The "synch" frame signals all potential receivers that a message is coming and provides a reference that can be used for each receiver to synchronize its clock to the clock of the transmitter. The "remote address" frame defines the station to which the message is sent. Eight bits (one "octet") allow one of any 256 stations to be identified. The "function" frame defines which of up to 256 different message types this one will be. An example might be "Turn off all of the following motors." The "internal address" frame describes which sets of registers within the receiving station the message is directed to. The "modifier" modifies the internal address and defines how many data words are included in the message. "Special Orders" contains shorthand messages about MTU and RTU conditions. An example might be "Reset all communication error counters." "Data" is a field of variable length, from 0 to 192 bits. "CRC" is a sixteen-bit cyclic redundancy code based on the Bose Chaudhuri Hocquenguem (BCH) formula for detecting transmission errors.

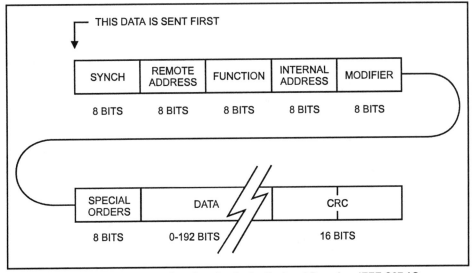

Figure 6-8. Layout of a Message Sent in a Particular Protocol Based on IEEE C37.1O

This is a good place to talk about the "CRC." As just mentioned, it is a code word that is calculated according to a formula. As with protocols, several CRC formulas can be used. In addition, as with protocols, it is vital to have the same CRC at both the sending and the receiving end. The CRC used in the sample protocol in Figure 6-8 is called the "(255,239) BCH." Two hundred fifty-five is the number of bits in the maximum-sized word that the code will guard. Two hundred thirty-nine is the number of bits of information (not including the CRC). As mentioned, *BCH* are the initials of the developers of the code, Bose, Chaudhuri, and Hocquenguem. Other codes that are used in industrial communications include CRC-16 and CRC-CCITT. The polynomial for (255,239) BCH is $(X^{16} + X^{14} + X^{13} + X^{11} + X^{10} + X^9 + X^8 + X^6 + X^5 + X^1 + 1)$.

Figure 6-9 explains how the CRC is calculated for an eight-bit word. The procedure appears very complicated but is accomplished quickly and easily by digital logic. Some methods start with sixteen bits of zeros rather than sixteen bits of ones. Some methods that transmit bits from right to left require that the polynomial be transformed left to right and the shifting be done to the right. When one station, either the MTU or the RTU, must send a message to another, it activates a part of itself called a protocol driver and uses that driver to encode the message into the form shown in Figure 6-8. The driver takes operational information and arranges it by the strict rules of the protocol. It checks to ensure that the communications link is clear. If it is, it passes a "request to send" to the next communications component, the modem.

PROCEDURE FOR CALCULATING A CYCLIC REDUNDANCY CODE

In this example, we will determine the CRC for an eight-bit data word, 0100 0000.

The CRC we will use is the (225,239) BCH, which has the generator polynomial of ($x^{16} + x^{14} + x^{13} + x^{11} + x^{10} + x^9 + x^8 + x^6 + x^5 + x + 1$). This can be rationalized to a binary word by placing a one in each of the identified bits and a zero in those not identified in the generator polynomial. The result is 1011 0111 1011 0001 1. Note that this is a 17-bit word. The most significant bit is discarded because it will not affect the arithmetic we will use it for. The effect polynomial is, then, the 16-bit word, 0110 1111 0110 0011.

The procedure looks complex but is easily handled by electronic binary logic.

A 16-bit register is filled with all ones. The data word is added to it, and simple shifts and additions are completed as follows.

FLAG	BINARY NUMBER	COMMENTS
	1111 1111 1111 1111	Initiate 16-bit register of all ones.
	0100 0000	First eight bits of the message.
	1011 1111 1111 1111	Sum of the two lines with no carrys, (exclusive OR).
1	0111 1111 1111 1110	Shift all bits one to the left. Note the flag is one.
	0110 1111 0110 0011	Since flag was one, add the polynomial.
	0001 0000 1001 1101	Sum of the two lines with no carrys, (exclusive OR).
0	0010 0001 0011 1010	Shift all bits one to the left. Note the flag is zero.
0	0100 0010 0111 0100	Since flag was zero, shift one bit to the left.
0	1000 0100 1110 1000	Since flag was zero, shift one bit to the left.
1	0000 1001 1101 0000	Since flag was zero, shift one bit to the left.
	0110 1111 0110 0011	Since flag was one, add the polynomial.
	0110 0110 1011 0011	Sum of the two lines with no carrys, (exclusive OR).
0	1100 1101 0110 1001	Shift all bits one to the left.
1	1001 1010 1101 0010	Since flag was zero, shift one bit to the left.
	0110 1111 0110 0011	Since flag was one, add the polynomial.
	1111 0101 1011 0001	Sum of the two lines with no carrys, (exclusive OR).
1	1110 1011 0110 0010	Shift all bits one to the left. If there were additional bits in the word, we would now add the next eight bits as we did the first eight and would go through the same process of adding the polynomial and shifting until we had made eight shifts. We would then add the next eight bits and so on.
		Since we are doing this example with only an eight-bit word, the process is complete. The CRC is the result after the eighth shift. It will be transmitted after the eight-bit data word, so the total message will be:
	0100 0000 1110 1011 0110 0010	
	I DATA I CRC I	

Figure 6-9. How the CRC Is Calculated for an Eight-bit Word

6-6.   Modems

The modem is at the lowest two levels in the ISO/OSI seven-layer model. It is the equipment that checks to determine if the communications medium is being used and turns the radio transmitter on. When all is ready, it changes the low-power binary signals as they are fed to it from the MTU or RTU into a form that will travel to the other end of the medium and be received by another modem. As noted in Unit 2, **mod**em is an acronym for "**mod**ulate and **dem**odulate." But what does "modulate" mean? Generally, it means to vary or to change a carrier wave according to a pattern.

Early attempts to send direct-current (DC) signals long distances over wireline demonstrated, not very surprisingly, that resistance reduced the signal. Attempts to send more and more pulses per second down the line demonstrated that inductance and capacitance effects also affected the signals. Limits to data rate and distance were reached early because the shape of the pulses was affected.

Figure 6-10 shows that a wave form can be separated mathematically into a series of sine waves. A French mathematician named Fourier described the method for analyzing this phenomenon. It turns out that sharp-edged pulses contain more high-frequency components than do round-edged pulses. The inductive reactance of a long pair of wires will selectively attenuate the high-frequency components, effectively rounding off the pulse, as in Figure 6-11.

In addition to this "amplitude distortion," the delay time imposed on component frequencies varies. Some frequency components take longer to get to the end of the line than others. This results in "phase distortion." A sine wave is immune to these forms of distortion. Resistance does decrease its amplitude, but the decrease is uniform over the entire wave. Because there is only one frequency, phase and amplitude distortion do not exist. For this reason, a sine wave is usually used as the carrier wave.

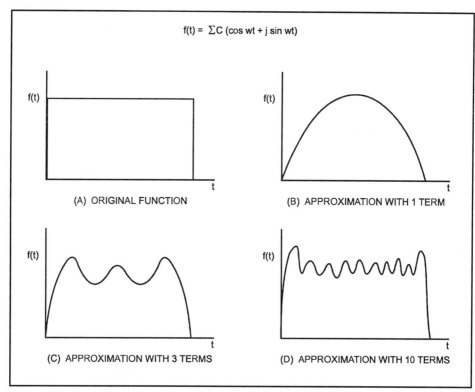

$$f(t) = \Sigma C (\cos wt + j \sin wt)$$

(A) ORIGINAL FUNCTION

(B) APPROXIMATION WITH 1 TERM

(C) APPROXIMATION WITH 3 TERMS

(D) APPROXIMATION WITH 10 TERMS

Figure 6-10. Wave Forms Can Be Separated into a Series of Sine Waves

The communications modulator varies one of three characteristics of the carrier. It may change the amplitude, the frequency, or the phase. "Amplitude modulation" (AM) varies the amplitude of the relatively high-frequency carrier by multiplying it by the amplitude of the data. The result is a series of sine waves at the carrier frequency that vary in amplitude at the data rate. See Figure 6-12. "Frequency modulation" (FM) varies the frequency of the carrier according to the amplitude of the data. Output amplitude is constant. Figure 6-13 shows the effect. Because most atmospheric noise is amplitude related and FM does not receive any intelligence from the signal amplitude, FM signals are not affected by atmospheric noise as much as are AM signals.

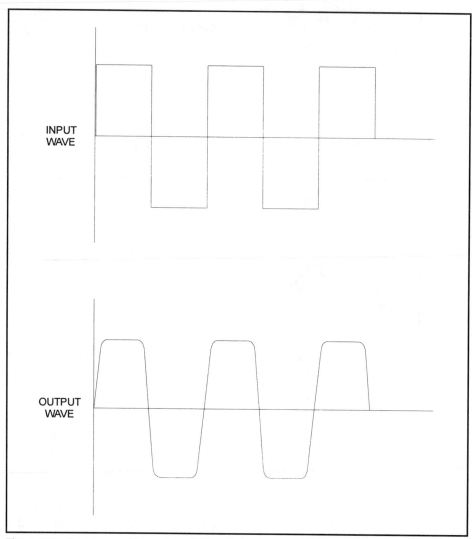

Figure 6-11. Reactance of Long Pair of Wires Selectively Attenuating the High-frequency Components

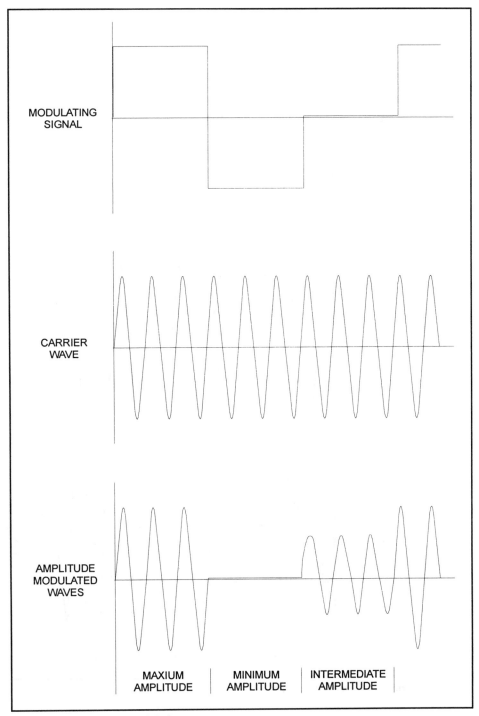

Figure 6-12. Amplitude Modulation

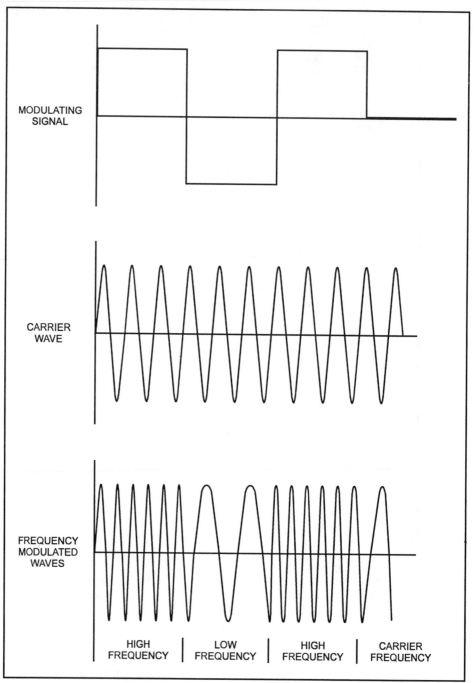

Figure 6-13. Frequency Modulation

"Phase modulation" (PM), also called "phase-shift keying" (PSK), involves changing the phase angle of the carrier wave in response to a change in the amplitude of the data. As the data rate approaches the carrier rate, PM looks more and more like FM. Quadra-phase modulation and other higher phase modulation modes allow data rates to exceed the carrier rate, creating the interesting situation in which a 2400 bps modem operates on a 1200-baud line. Demodulators are devices that take a modulated signal, strip the carrier from it, and are left with the data. They then pass this data up to the protocol driver to have the data distributed to the proper registers in the receiving station.

6-7.   Synchronous or Asynchronous?

Synchronous and asynchronous refer to the need for a timing signal to be transmitted with the data. Synchronous modems must transmit a clock pulse that is used to ensure that the receiver is working at the same clock speed as the transmitter. Usually, the transmitted clock is used to synchronize a clock at the receiver. In other cases, the transmitted clock is conditioned and actually becomes the clock signal at the receiver. Both of these methods cause the clock signals at the transmitter and receiver to have the same phase and frequency relationship.

Asynchronous modems do not require that the receiver be clock-synchronized with the transmitter. "Start of message" and "end of message" signals are required to advise the asynchronous receiver of the status of a message.

6-8.   Telephone Cable or Radio?

The communications medium used by the SCADA system is determined by two things: data rate and cost.

We developed a method that calculated the scan interval in Unit 4. The method was based on several things, including the data rate, and trade-offs could be made between the data rate and scan interval. For some SCADA purposes, it is not feasible to get a short enough scan interval unless the data rate is pushed very high, that is, over 5000 bps. When this situation exists, a communications medium with a bandwidth greater than a voice-grade line will be required, such as optical fiber cable, microwave radio, or one of the more sophisticated UHF systems. Lines leased from the telephone company are one possibility for this communications medium. The cost is likely to be fairly high, but for those industries that require high-volume, high-speed data, these choices do exist.

When an acceptable scan interval can be achieved with data rates in the 300 to 4800 bps range, the choice becomes much broader. All of the preceding solutions will meet the technical requirements. In addition, other equipment that will do the job are a voice-grade telephone line, which is designed to operate from 300 to 3400 Hz, or inexpensive UHF radios designed for commercial and light industrial applications.

Telephone cable was at one time the preferred communications medium. The low cost of purchasing and installing it made its use acceptable, but some problems had to be solved first. Problems caused by rodents chewing through the cable were eliminated by putting armor around the conductors. Figure 6-14 shows a buried cable construction cutaway. Various materials have been successfully used to keep water out of the cable, but efforts to keep ditchers from digging the cable up have been unsuccessful. The cost of installation dropped when a cable construction technique was developed that allowed direct ploughing. Solid rock must be blasted to provide a trench. Purchasing right-of-way in which to bury the cable is sometimes very expensive. The cable signals can be affected by high currents in parallel power transmission lines and by low-frequency magnetic effects from sunspot activity.

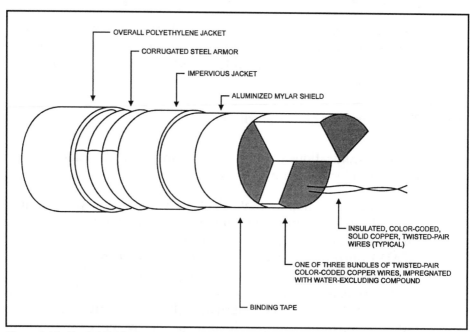

Figure 6-14. Buried Cable Construction Cutaway

For remote areas, where telephone companies do not have an incentive to install their own lines, it may be necessary for the user to pay a high capital cost to get the telephone company to install a line that can be leased. In other areas, the user may have to purchase and install the cable. Optical fiber cable is becoming cost competitive with copper, even for small, low-data-rate links. It can be ploughed in or installed in the same trench as a new pipeline. Any cable will have the disadvantage of inflexibility. When it is in, it stays in; one cannot decide five years later that it would be nice to move it. For many applications, however, this permanence is not a problem.

Radio communications will be discussed in detail in Unit 7. UHF radios have been developed specifically for SCADA. They offer flexibility, low cost, and high reliability. The issues that surround licenses for new frequencies are discussed in Unit 7 and so will not be reiterated here. Figure 6-15 shows a remote site with a radio communications package for sending low-speed data to an MTU about fifteen kilometers away.

Communications is the key to a SCADA system. It is much more dependent than any other major SCADA element on the conditions found at the area where the SCADA is installed. For this reason, communications deserves a great deal of attention at the early stages of design.

Exercises:

6-1. *For low-speed SCADA, what two common media are used?*

6-2. *Name the three methods for modulating a sine wave.*

6-3. *What is a cyclic redundancy code (CRC) used for? Is it calculated by the MTU or the RTU? How many bits does it usually have?*

6-4. *Is it possible to transmit more than 1200 bps on a 1200-baud modem?*

6-5. *How many pairs of wire are in a buried telephone line?*

6-6. *What equipment is needed to send an analog signal from an RTU to an MTU?*

6-7. *What does a protocol driver do?*

6-8. *As part of the communications procedure, one piece of equipment is responsible for checking if the communications medium is in use. What is that equipment called?*

Figure 6-15. Remote Terminal Unit with Radio (Courtesy: Spartan Controls Ltd.)

Unit 7: Radio

UNIT 7

Radio

Radio is the most complex of the two types of communication commonly used in SCADA systems. For this reason, we will devote this entire unit to elucidating its intricacies.

Learning Objectives — When you have completed this unit, you should:

A.   Know the basic vocabulary of radio communications.

B.   Understand the common problems associated with radio.

C.   Be able to determine what kind of radio communications package is required for your SCADA system.

7-1.   Simplex or Duplex?

Communication can be a one-way pass of information or a two-way exchange. Earlier in this text, we determined that for both the supervisory control function and the data acquisition functions to be realized the information in a SCADA system must move in both directions. The terms used to describe the ability of a communications system to move information are as follows: simplex, half duplex, and duplex or full duplex. These terms refer to other communications systems besides radio, but to appreciate how radio systems are selected it is important that you understand what they mean.

Simplex systems, shown in Figure 7-1, allow information to be passed in one direction. Paul Revere used a simplex system when he lit a lamp to indicate "One if by land, two if by sea." He could send the information out but could receive no information back. Even the information that his message had been received was not immediately available to him. Amerind smoke signals (when only one fire was used) were also simplex communications. They sent the information out but did not receive information back. Note that the addition of a second fire would change the system status from simplex to something else.

More recent examples of simplex systems are the various signals sent by telemetry from weather balloons, experimental rockets, and commercial radio and TV broadcasts. Since SCADA requires two-way movement of information, it does not use simplex communication.

Figure 7-1. Simplex Systems

At the other end of the communications utility spectrum is duplex (sometimes called "full duplex" for reasons that will soon become evident). Duplex communication allows information to be transmitted and received at the same time. Duplex is like having two simplex systems running parallel to each other but in opposite directions (see Figure 7-2). The **du**-part of the word derives from the fact that duplex systems allow full **two**-way communication. An early example is semaphore, which used a sender and a receiver at each end of the path. Each of the stations can thus both "talk" and "listen." More recent technology-based examples of duplex include the telephone. But while full duplex offers an advantage in terms of utility, it comes at the cost of requiring more wires or other equipment than simplex.

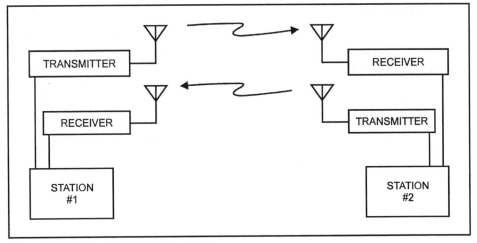

Figure 7-2. Duplex or Full Duplex System

Interestingly, a compromise is available. If it is necessary to move information in both directions but not continuously, it is possible to use one pair of wires or one radio frequency with the data going sometimes in one direction, sometimes in the other. This is called half duplex. As Figure 7-3 shows, some additional switching is necessary. It wouldn't do, for example, to have the transmitter output connected to the receiver input.

SCADA systems are able to use either full duplex or half duplex. The criteria for selection are not exclusively the cost of an extra pair of wires in a land line cable or an extra crystal for a radio. They may include the time it takes for a radio transmitter to turn on and stabilize or the availability of an extra radio frequency in a limited spectrum that has great demands on it.

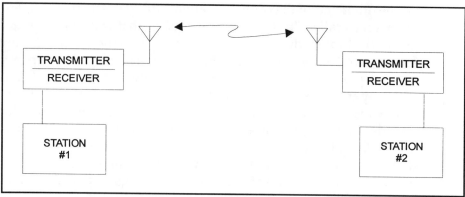

Figure 7-3. Half Duplex System

7-2.   Turn-On Time

Figure 7-4 illustrates a typical SCADA radio system that consists of one MTU and five RTUs. It would be possible for the MTU to (1) send a message to its radio to start transmitting, (2) wait until the radio transmitter settled down, (3) modulate the transmitter with the message it wanted sent to RTU number 1, including the RTU 1 identification, (4) turn the radio transmitter off, then (5) turn its receiver on and wait for RTU 1 to answer.

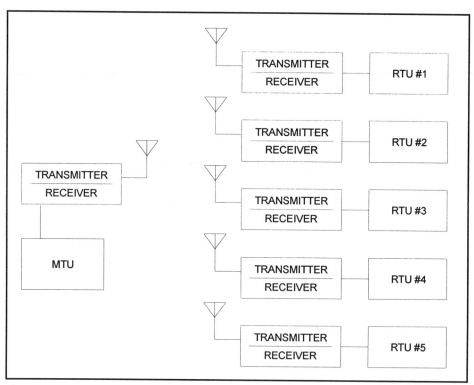

Figure 7-4. Typical SCADA Radio System

All of the RTUs would normally wait with their receivers on. When a message is received, the message is checked to see if the message is for RTU 1 or some other RTU. If it is not for RTU 1, RTU 1 will ignore it. If it is for RTU 1, it will be acted on within the RTU. Then RTU passes a message back to the MTU by turning its receiver off, turning its transmitter on, waiting until the transmitter settles down, modulating the radio carrier with the message (which includes its identification), turning the transmitter off, and turning the receiver on.

At first glance, the transmitter turn-on step does not look very significant. When a timing chart, as shown in Figure 7-5, is drawn, it is obvious that the time it takes to turn the transmitter on can be significant. More than one half of the total transaction time can be used, but this will vary depending on message length and data rates. This is one of the factors that is used to calculate communication efficiency.

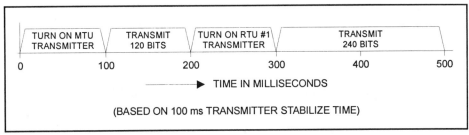

Figure 7-5. Timing Chart - 1200 Baud - Half Duplex

The length of the wait for radio transmitters to turn on and stabilize is a function of the radio and is generally independent of the data rate. Because of this, attempts to reduce the scan interval should concentrate not exclusively on data rate but also on the communications equipment. One way to improve the communications equipment is to take advantage of full duplex. If the second frequency is available, the MTU can transmit on one, and all the RTUs can transmit on the other (see Figure 7-6). The implication is that the MTU radio can transmit 100 percent of the time; therefore, it is not necessary to wait for it to stabilize each time a message is sent from the MTU. Most of the time, only the carrier will be transmitted by the MTU. This technique is often used and results in a shortening of scan rate for a small increase in cost. Since all the RTUs are using the same frequency to transmit, only one can transmit at a time. For radio communications, it is seldom justified to have each RTU transmit on a separate frequency.

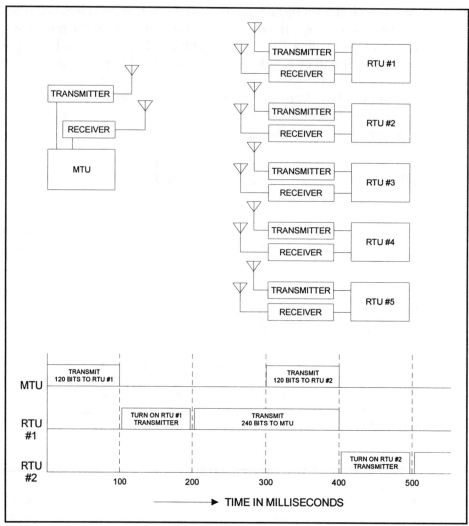

Figure 7-6. Full Duplex with Second Frequency Available

7-3.   Frequencies: Are They Available?

Earlier in this unit we showed that by adding one frequency (essentially doubling the requirement) we could effect an improvement in the response of a SCADA system. But that improvement was also accompanied by the caution, "If the second frequency is available ..."

As with many other things is this world, radio frequencies are commodities that are in demand and are being used up. People think of the number of frequencies as being limitless, but that is also the way people used to think of the dodo and carrier pigeons. When radio is chosen as the medium for SCADA communications, some limitations automatically exist. One of these is that simplex not only needs one frequency; it also requires a band of frequencies centered around the one carrier frequency. The width of this band, or bandwidth, is related to the modulation rate (measured in baud) that we wish to use. Depending on the type of modulation, the bandwidth in Hz is about equal to the number of bits per second for single sideband AM, which is about two times the number of bits per second for FSK (frequency-shift keying) modulation and three times the number of bits per second for FM (frequency modulation). Phase-shift modulation can actually move data at a rate higher than the baud rate, but even then a significant amount of bandwidth is required.

In addition to this bandwidth, a guard band of several hundred Hz is added above and below the band being used. This guard band prevents the overlap of frequencies and the resulting interference when (not if) the radio transmitter drifts off the frequency it is calibrated to use. Therefore, to communicate at 1200 bps, a band of frequencies about 3000 Hz wide is required. Interestingly enough, this is just about the same bandwidth needed to communicate analog voice data with acceptable quality. Could it be that 1200 bps has become a standard for this reason?

The other factor that limits how many frequencies (or frequency bands) are available for use is their range. Some people can remember listening to commercial radio at night and being bothered by unfamiliar stations drifting in and out. Sometimes this interference was so strong that it completely obscured the information being listened to. This phenomenon can be described by stating that the signal-to-noise ratio (SNR) has dropped below 1. When listening to the radio for enjoyment this is a nuisance. When a SCADA RTU is listening to the radio to receive an order to block in a leaking oil pipeline and the SNR drops below 1, it is much more than just a nuisance.

Radio waves refract and reflect for many reasons, but, generally, higher frequencies refract less than lower frequencies. There is a group of frequencies between 300 MHz and 3000 MHz called UHF (ultrahigh frequency). It has the benefits of being limited (nearly) to line of sight and yet is still technically simple enough to be maintainable in the field. Most SCADA radio operates in the UHF range. The International Telecommunications Union (ITU), a United Nations agency, organizes World Administrative Radio Conferences to allocate bands of frequencies on a worldwide basis. The decisions of these conferences are binding on the member countries and are used to establish national regulations.

Government regulatory agencies carefully evaluate applications to use frequencies and allocate those frequencies if they are available and if the agency is convinced that the applicant really needs them. It is not a foregone conclusion that a license will be issued just because an application is made.

7-4.   Path Studies and Seasonal Variations

As the frequency gets higher, the radio waves act more and more like light. At the UHF band, and even more so for microwave radio (which is sometimes used for high-data-rate SCADA), the radio path is essentially line-of-sight. One of the implications of this is that the system design must include a "path study." For each link between transmitter and receiver, an evaluation must be made regarding transmitter power, antenna gain, losses as a function of distance, and, very importantly, whether any hills lie between the transmitter and the receiver. The path study uses topographical maps, which may suggest changes of location that will keep antenna tower heights to a minimum or indicate the need for radio repeater stations. Figure 7-7 shows a simplified path study.

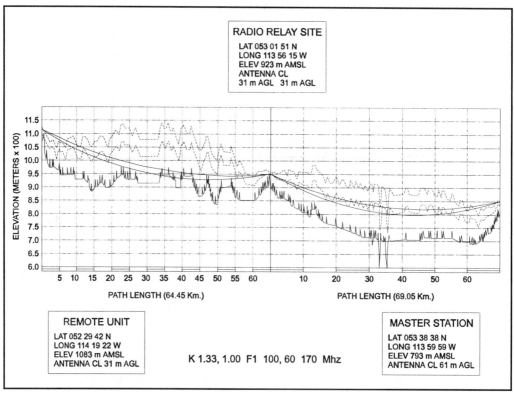

Figure 7-7. Simplified Path Study (Courtesy: ParaDimensions Inc.)

Sometimes the safety margin for path studies is shaved thin to keep the costs of antenna towers or repeater stations down. There have been cases in which a system worked well during the winter months, but when springtime brought leaves to the trees on a hill between the transmitter and receiver the signal level dropped down into the noise. Some coniferous trees have needles that act as one-quarter wavelength antennas, absorbing much of the incident radio power.

7-5.   Solar Variations

Radio signals propagate through space as electromagnetic waves and are indistinguishable from other electromagnetic waves of the same frequency. One of the reasons why it takes a long time to get a radio license is that the agency responsible for issuing it must check whether the applicant will interfere with another receiver on that frequency and must ensure that no other transmitter on that frequency will interfere with the applicant.

But this cannot prevent the most powerful radiator in the neighborhood from transmitting radio noise periodically. Every eleven years, the sun experiences a major series of storms that are accompanied by sunspots and flares. The affect on radio traffic is very damaging. UHF and microwave are less affected by solar variations than some of the other bands, but even they may see increased amounts of noise. The best ways to minimize the effects of solar radio activity are to design initially for a high SNR (Signal to Noise Ratio) and to keep the equipment maintained and calibrated.

7-6.   Reliability and Maintenance

Solid-state electronics has made improvements in radio technology that could not have been imagined twenty years ago. Of course, the first thing that most people think of when such a statement is made is that the equipment is now smaller and uses less power. That, in fact, is true. But what is probably more important is that reliability and maintainability have been improved. Figure 7-8 shows a radio modem designed especially for SCADA applications.

Temperature compensation is now built in. Immunity to vibration and power supply transients is much better. But some maintenance of radio equipment is still required. Antennas loosened by the wind and shifted ninety degrees from their intended target must be realigned. The electric storage cells of uninterruptible power supplies (UPS), which ensure that the radios receive continuous electrical power, must be cleaned and refilled from time to time. Even the radios themselves can be damaged by lightning or can drift and thus require checking and repair. But they are much better now than they were.

Figure 7-8. RTU with Built-In Modem (Left) and Built-For-Purpose Radio (Right) (Courtesy: Imperial Oil Resources Ltd.)

7-7. Satellite Communications

Geosynchronous communications satellites are now at the threshold of affordability for SCADA communications. For most applications, there are less expensive ways to send messages back and forth between MTU and RTUs. But for very large systems such as pipelines and electric transmission lines, especially in remote, poorly developed areas, such satellites may be the most cost-effective communications method.

The principle is simple. The MTU and each of the RTUs have access to an antenna that is pointed at a satellite that stays over the same spot (hence, geosynchronous). The satellite acts as a radio repeater, receiving data from one station and sending it to the others. Usually, a capital cost must be paid for the antennas and special radio equipment. There is also a monthly fee for the service. This is much like the tariff charged for any utility communications equipment. The costs are becoming more reasonable as more users share the systems, which, of course, have very high start-up costs.

Although radio systems appear to have many drawbacks, they usually offer sufficient advantages over land lines to make them the medium of choice.

Exercises:

7-1.   *Why is simplex communication not used for SCADA?*

7-2.   *The pony express system used a series of horses and riders to move letters both east and west but only in one direction at a time. Was this simplex, duplex, or half duplex?*

7-3.   *Why is transmitter turn-on time something to be avoided?*

7-4.   *Master-slave protocols allow the slaves to transmit only after they have been told to do so. Assuming that all of the RTUs (slaves) transmit to the MTU on one frequency, what would be the effect if one RTU transmitter stuck in the transmit mode? Describe a cost-effective way to prevent this problem.*

7-5.   *Frequency-shift keying (FSK) and phase-shift modulation are two popular modulation techniques for moving binary data. Why?*

7-6.   *UHF radios have some advantages over lower-frequency equipment; for example, the antennae needed to focus the signal can be made much smaller for UHF. What is one of the disadvantages of UHF?*

7-7.   *Sunspot activity sends streams of charged particles into the Earth's magnetic field. What effects can be expected from this?*

7-8.   *Name nine improvements in the radios used for SCADA in the past twenty years.*

Unit 8:
Remote Terminal Units (RTUs)

UNIT 8

Remote Terminal Units (RTUs)

Aside from the communications equipment, a SCADA system is characterized by two other elements, the remote terminal units (RTUs) and the master terminal units (MTUs). In Unit 2 we briefly discussed what RTUs and MTUs are and what they do. In this unit, we will go into more detail about the RTU.

Learning Objectives — When you have completed this unit, you should:

A. Understand what an RTU does, how it does it, and why.

B. Know how this element fits into a general SCADA package and how it interfaces with the process and with the communications link.

8-1. What Does an RTU Do?

In Unit 1, we discussed the RTU's functionality in terms of a "black box" that accomplished some poorly defined functions. Figure 8-1 shows what signals come into the RTU in block form; Figure 8-2 shows what signals leave the RTU. To review them briefly, the RTU gathers information from the field about analog values, alarm and status points, and metered amounts. It keeps this information available in memory until the MTU asks for it. It then codes and transmits the information to the MTU. In addition, when the MTU instructs, the RTU opens and closes valves, turns switches on and off, outputs analog signals that may represent set points, and outputs pulse trains to move stepping motors. This may seem like a rather limited repertoire of functions, but it is sufficient to accomplish all the remote control and monitoring that needs to be done.

RTUs are now being offered that have the ability to receive and send messages to field devices in serial format, usually RS-232. In most cases, this feature does not increase SCADA's functionality. however, it does simplify some of the field local data transfer. In the near future, we can expect that serial communications in the form of fieldbus will outnumber the 4-20 mA analog signals used now. At the time this is written, fieldbus is just starting to appear in process control designs. Its advantages, particularly for small systems, are so solid that it will clearly become the protocol of choice for field installations in SCADA systems.

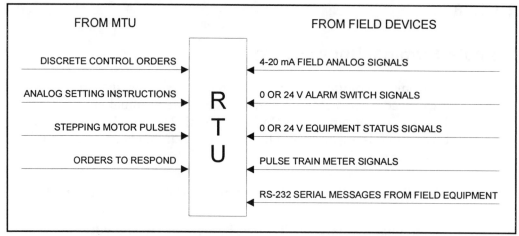

Figure 8-1. The Signals That Come into the RTU

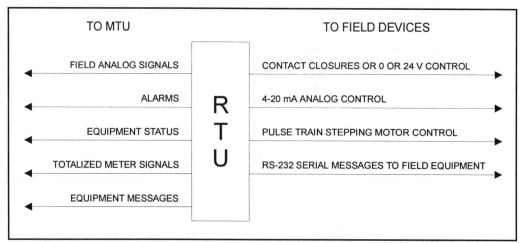

Figure 8-2. The Signals That Leave the RTU

8-2.   Communications Interface

Figure 8-3 expands the black box description of an RTU. Modern RTUs are essentially microcomputers with special equipment at one end that is designed to interface with the communications link and with special equipment at the other end to interface with the sensors, actuators, and calculators in the process. While the RTU is in receive mode, part of the communications interface equipment (the modem) receives a serial signal from the communications medium. This signal is conditioned to a stream of bits that are either ones or zeros. At this stage, the signal is not analog, although some analog signals may have been coded into binary for transmission to the RTU. Using rules that were established when the communications protocol was developed, another part of the communications interface interprets the string of ones and zeros and passes the information on to the rest of the RTU.

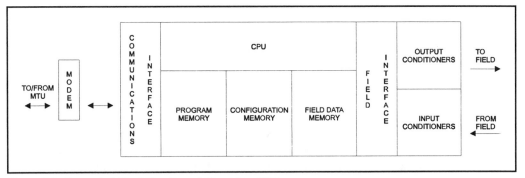

Figure 8-3. Expanded Black Box Description of an RTU

Note that in some cases the interpretation function is accomplished by the microprocessor that forms the heart of the RTU. When this type of architecture is used, part of the program that translates the ones and zeros into useful information is called a "protocol driver" program. Also, for this architecture, the interrupt feature, which is critical to the operation of an RTU, must execute quickly or there must be a buffer to store the incoming message. If the first bit or bits of a message is not recognized the message is often not understood. The RTU does not know when a message is going to be sent to it. It must always be in the listening mode (except when it is transmitting). However, while it is listening the RTU will be doing many other things. Early RTUs used electronic circuits that were dedicated to listening continuously for incoming messages, decoding them, storing them in buffer memory, and passing pertinent information to the rest of the RTU when the RTU demanded it. Modern RTUs accomplish these functions with the protocol driver program run by the RTU's CPU (central processor unit).

8-3.   Protocol Detailed

Protocol was discussed in Unit 6, but it may be useful to use an example to review how a simple message is received and decoded at the RTU. Recall that the information is received at the modem located at the RTU as a series of ones and zeros modulated onto a carrier frequency. The modem strips off the carrier and makes a series of ones and zeros available to the RTU. For the purposes of this discussion, the protocol will be one based on ANSI/IEEE C37.1-1979. Many other protocols exist, however, and the selection of this particular protocol is not important to this discussion.

What is important is that you learn how much detail there is in a protocol definition.

In Figure 8-4 (and all other figures like it) the leftmost bit of information is the first one received. Figure 8-4 shows the three basic fields in the binary message. They are "message establishment," "information," and "message termination." For the example shown in the figure, message establishment and message termination have fixed lengths. Information fields may be of different lengths.

The "message establishment" field has two subfields, as shown in Figure 8-5. The first is called "Sync" (for synchronizing) and is one "octet" or eight bits long (00010100). It establishes that an MTU is sending a message to an RTU. This subfield is also used to synchronize the RTU clock to the MTU clock. The second subfield, the "Remote Address," defines which RTU the MTU is sending the message to. It also consists of eight bits. Normally, eight bits would allow two-to-the-eighth-power or 256 RTUs to be addressed, but only 254 of these addresses are valid (0 and 255 are reserved). The address in this figure, 00001011, decodes to RTU number 11. Unless both subfields are recognized, an RTU knows that the message is not addressed to it, ignores the rest of the message, and resets its message establishment registers to wait for another message. The RTU with the matching address listens for the next stage, which is "information."

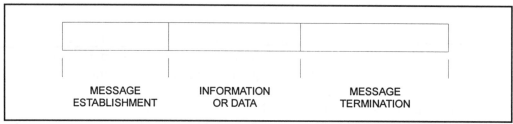

Figure 8-4. The Three Basic Fields in the Binary Message

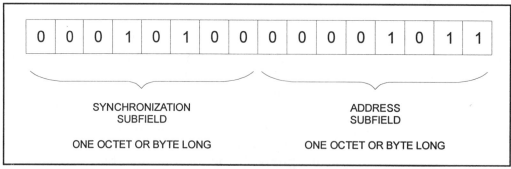

Figure 8-5. The "Message Establishment" Field Has Two Subfields

The "information" field shown in Figure 8-6 consists of several subfields of data that the MTU wants to pass to the RTU. The first subfield, "Function," defines the type of response that the RTU must make to this message or the type of control message that the MTU is now transmitting. There are eight bits in this subfield, so there are two-to-the-eighth-power or 256 potential responses that could be demanded and/or 256 control message types that could be sent. An example of a control message might be binary number seven, which could mean "Close all of the following valves." An example of a response demand message might be "Send the totalized flow values for fluid meters."

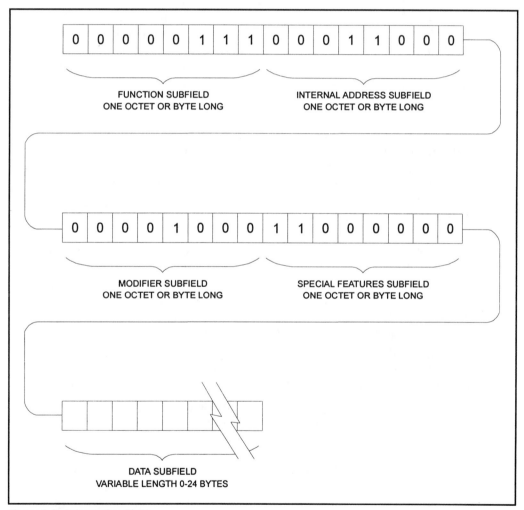

Figure 8-6. Information Field

The "Internal Address" subfield identifies the location within the RTU. For example, this subfield might say "24," meaning that memory register 24 is the location of the first of those fluid meter totals to be sent, or it might mean "The valve identified in memory register 24 is the first in the list of valves to close." The third subfield, "Modifier," defines the number of data units to be transferred. In this example, if the modifier were eight, the MTU would be asking that totals from meters 24 to 31 (24 + 8), inclusive, be sent. Or it might mean "The eight valves including and after the one identified in memory register 24 are the ones to close."

The fourth subfield, "Special Orders," allows for special instructions to the RTU, including resetting trouble flags, resetting communication error flags, and "Expect a long message at the next command." A one in the most-significant-bit position (left side) means that the MTU acknowledges that the RTU has executed a restart and instructs the RTU to reset this flag. A one in the second MSB means the MTU acknowledges that the RTU has detected a communication-related problem and instructs the RTU to reset this flag.

The "Expect a long message at the next command" flag deserves some explanation. Most SCADA systems do much more monitoring than they do controlling. For this reason, messages from the MTU to the RTU are usually shorter than messages from the RTU to the MTU (in this protocol). The MTU will alert an RTU when it is going to send a long message that includes data subfields to the RTU.

The fifth subfield, "Data," provides for generalized data to be sent from the MTU to the RTU. For a message of the type used in this example, the data subfield would have a length of zero. For other message types it could be up to twenty-four octets long. After the information field is complete, a "message terminator" field, which consists of one subfield, is included (see Figure 8-7). The first, called "Security Code," consists of sixteen bits that are calculated at the MTU based on the information sent from the MTU. This sixteen-bit number is compared to a sixteen-bit number calculated by the RTU based on the data it receives. If the two sixteen-bit numbers are identical, the message is assumed to have been received correctly. The algorithm that is used is a cyclic redundancy code (CRC), which we discussed in Unit 6.

When the entire message has been received and confirmed as correct, the RTU, in addition to all of the other things it has been doing, will perform the instructions contained in the message just received. This last message required that a certain group of fluid meter volumes contained in registers 24 to 31 be sent to the MTU. The RTU will now refer to its memory registers, pull out the appropriate information, develop a message to the MTU according to similar rules and using the same protocol, and tell the MTU what those registers contain.

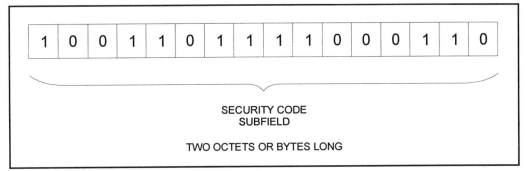

Figure 8-7. Message Terminator Field

8-4.   Discrete Control

Many of the messages from the MTU relate to control. They will require
the RTU to develop and transfer a signal to one of the field elements near
its location. In this section, we'll first follow the activities that occur if a
message is received by the RTU calling for it to open a two-position valve,
when the first valve location in memory is memory location 32 and the
number of valves is two. See Figure 8-8.

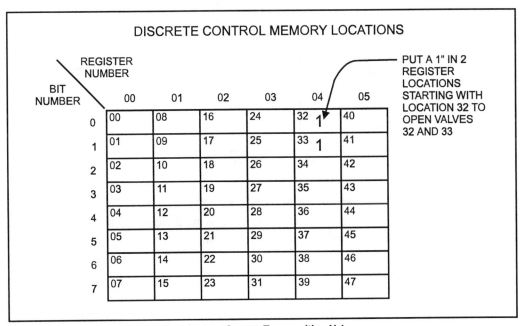

Figure 8-8. Message to RTU Calling for It to Open a Two-position Valve

The RTU will locate the registers that are allocated to controlling discrete valves. Notice that since each register is one octet or eight bits long and each bit is able to define "closed" position by "0" and "open" position by "1" each register can control eight discrete elements. The RTU will locate the first specified register position (position 32 in register 04) and force it to a "1" state. It will then move to the second position (33) and force it to a "1" state. A couple of milliseconds later this register is routinely read (see Figure 8-9). At this point, because these two registers have a "1" in their positions they will cause two control buffer register positions to go to a "1." A "1" on these positions will cause two relay drivers on an output card to latch two relays closed. Each of these relays will drive a solenoid valve that will allow instrument air to open one of the valves. Notice that the latching, either at the relay driver or the relay itself, causes the control to be "Fail to last position." This means that if the communications system fails after the message has been received to open the valves the valves will stay open. If it becomes necessary to close them while the SCADA system is out of service, a manual or safety instrumented system that acts to override the SCADA must be put in place.

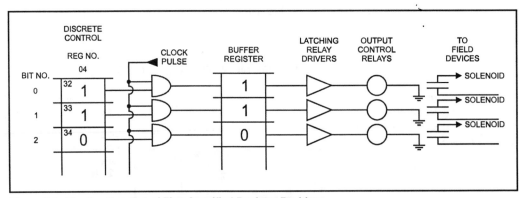

Figure 8-9. Routine Reading of First Specified Register Position

The same procedure would be used to turn a motor on. Instead of energizing a solenoid, the latching relay would close a motor starter. Most discrete binary controls can be effected this way.

8-5. Analog Control

Suppose the MTU instructed the RTU to open a valve, not all the way but only to 75 percent of wide open. This would be handled by an analog control instruction. For this example, shown in Figure 8-10, the MTU message will call for analog output, register number 22, and set it at +75 percent. In this case, it takes more than one bit to define the requirement. Register 22 has eight bits, the same number register 04 had in the last example. Now, however, more data is required to define the degree of openness of the valve. Eight bits will allow one part in 2^8, or one in 256, which is about 1/2 percent. For many control situations this is adequate, and eight bits of precision are usually used. Applications that need more precision control use part or all of a second eight-bit register. Sixteen bits results in a precision of one in two to the power of sixteen, or one in 65,536. For this example, eight bits of the twenty-second analog register have been set 11000000, which is 75 percent of 256.

	ANALOG CONTROL REGISTER NUMBER 22	BIT VALUE
BIT 0	1	50%
BIT 1	1	25%
BIT 2	0	12.5%
BIT 3	0	6.25%
BIT 4	0	3.125%
BIT 5	0	1.5625%
BIT 6	0	0.78125%
BIT 7	0	0.390625%

Figure 8-10. MTU Message Calls for Analog Output, Register 22

Now, when the clock strobe pulse comes by and these values are moved to a buffer register, something different will happen. In an analog output card (Figure 8-11), these bits must be reconstituted into an analog signal. For this exercise, assume that 10 volts will cause the valve to go 100 percent open, and 0 volts will cause it to go 0 percent open. The first bit (called bit 0) is the most significant bit (MSB). Because it is a one, it turns on a voltage source that outputs 5 volts. The second bit (called bit 1) because it is also a one turns on a voltage source that outputs 2.5 volts. The third bit (called bit 2) because it is a zero does not turn on the 1.25-volt voltage source. The fourth also does not turn on the 0.625 volt source and so on. All of these voltages are added, and the resulting 7.5 volts is fed to a power driver. From here it may be turned into a 4-20 mA signal. This would result in $(0.75 \times (20 - 4) + 4) = 16$ mA being sent to a valve so as to position the valve at 75 percent of full open position.

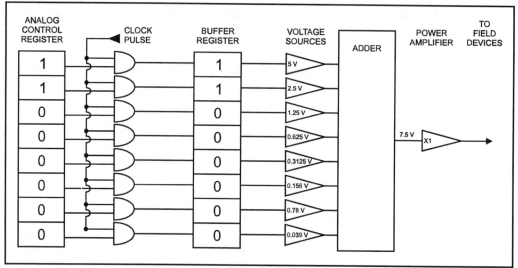

Figure 8-11. Analog Output Card

In fact, the signal would be more likely to act as the remote set point of a PID (proportional-integral-derivative) controller, and the output from the controller could control a valve, a louver, a machine speed, or any number of parameters that could be described by an analog value between 0 and 100 percent.

8-6.   Pulse Control

The pulse control method of control is seldom used and will not be discussed in detail here. It allows a stepper motor to be incremented or decremented by a specified number of steps. The sixteen-bit register may have the 0 bit set with a one to increment or a zero to decrement. One of the remaining fifteen bits will be set with a one for each pulse output that is required. Rather than clocking all bits out simultaneously from the buffer register, they are clocked out one at a time and arranged to go to the stepper motor one after another (serially).

One of the reasons this system is not popular is that each instruction to the motor requires a knowledge of the motor's initial position. In time, errors will accumulate in the supposed initial position of the motor. It therefore becomes necessary to intermittently force the motor either full open or full closed to reregister its position. While this is not particularly difficult from a control point of view, it can have some very destabilizing effects on the process.

Feedback position switches are now being applied to eliminate this problem, but the damage done by poor early applications makes this an unpopular method of control.

8-7.   Serial Control

Many end devices are equipped with serial input and output capability. This capability simplifies the movement of data between instrument registers and RTU registers.

8-8.   Monitor Discrete Signals

One of the most common data acquisition features that a SCADA system is called on to perform is the monitoring of discrete status or alarm points. These are sometimes called digital points. Consider Figure 8-12, which is the representation of a discrete alarm--in this case a high-level switch on a hydroelectric reservoir. The wiper side of the switch, LSH-101, is supplied with 24-volt DC from the RTU. When the water level gets high enough to open the switch, the return wire carrying the 24-volt signal has its voltage source interrupted to some signal conditioning circuitry. Here, transients, AC noise, and the effects of switch contact bounce are removed, and the voltage is shifted to a level more compatible with the logic level. A clock pulse transfers the conditioned signal, in this case a +5-volt level, into discrete input register number 20, bit 7, as a "1." The next time the MTU asks the RTU for the status of discrete input register 20, bit 7, the RTU will look at this bit and report that it is a "1." The MTU will then know that the water level in the reservoir is high.

Of course, if the water level had been low, the 24-volt signal would have continued to reach the signal conditioner, and the output of the signal conditioner would have been zero volts. This would have been clocked into the register as a "0." A "0" in discrete input register 20, bit 7, would be configured to mean that there is not a high level in the reservoir.

Discrete inputs can inform on the status of a vast range of parameters. Levels, pressures, temperatures, flows, valve positions, motor status, and so on can be monitored using simple switches. By using special logic with relay contact output, it is also possible to get the status of high-radiation monitors, combustible gas alarms, out-of-limits pH analysis, and nearly anything else.

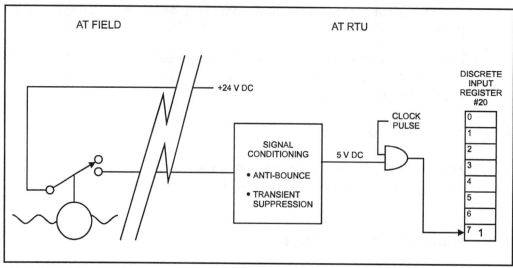

Figure 8-12. A Discrete Alarm

8-9.   Monitor Analog Signals

It is often important to monitor a process parameter to get more than a binary amount of information. For example, the actual height of liquid in the reservoir, the speed of a motor, or the level of radiation may be needed. In these situations a sensor is provided that changes the parameter of interest to a more easily monitored quantity, such as current.

In Figure 8-13, the float on the surface of the reservoir modifies the 24-volt DC supplied by the RTU so that, over the range that interests us, the current varies from 4 mA to 20 mA. This current, fed through a 250-ohm resistor, results in a voltage of between 1 volt and 5 volts at the input of the circuit, which does some signal conditioning and then samples and holds the voltage. An analog-to-digital converter (ADC) then operates on the voltage. A detailed description of how this works was given in Section 6.2. The result is an eight-bit word that represents the 1 volt to 5 volts to within about 1/2 percent. If better accuracy were needed, and it seldom is, up to sixteen bits could be employed. This word is clocked into a specific register, and the RTU, when asked, will send the contents of the register to the MTU.

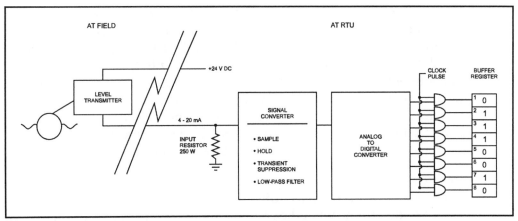

Figure 8-13. Float on the Surface of a Reservoir Modifies 24-volt DC Supplied by the RTU

8-10. Monitor Pulse Count Signals

Many sensors or local instruments that originally output their information from odometer-style readouts have been modified to be read by SCADA. Often, the least expensive way is to have the device send a string of pulses or interrupt a current from the RTU by opening and closing a relay contact in such a way that each open-close cycle represents a fixed, known amount. In this way, the RTU can count or accumulate these contact closures and infer from their sum how much the device has measured. Figure 8-14 shows how such a device works.

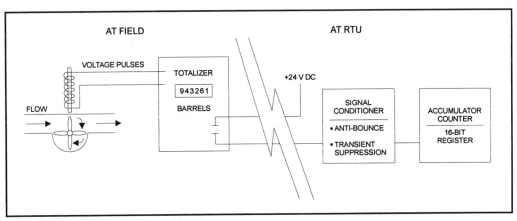

Figure 8-14. Monitor Pulse Count Signals

A totalizer, which is a device external to the RTU, outputs a contact closure for each barrel of oil that passes through a turbine meter. This contact closure is energized by the 24-volt DC from the RTU, and the intermittent signal is fed into a signal conditioner, complete with transient suppression and antibounce circuitry. In this case, however, the output from the signal conditioner is passed into a counting circuit that is composed of flip-flops and steering logic. Typically, the counter will have sixteen bits and so can count up to two-to-the-sixteenth-power (65,536) engineering units. Some RTUs include totalizer functionality internal to themselves.

This number should be used at the design stage, in conjunction with the scan period and the degree of difficulty of sending an operator to the facility, to determine what the engineering units should be. For this example, the engineering unit represented by one count could be 1/1000 of a barrel, 1/10 of a barrel, 1 barrel, or 100 barrels. If the oil well produced about 65 barrels of oil per hour and the scan period were one hour, it would be poor design to have each count represent 1/1000 barrel. There would be cases where there was uncertainty, from one scan to the next, whether the well had produced 10/10,000 or (675,536 + 10)/10,000 of a barrel. It would be better to have each register bit represent 1/100 of a barrel or even 1/10 of a barrel. Then, several hours of power failure and a few consecutive communications errors would still give you enough time to send an operator to the RTU to manually read the total before the counter rolls over to zero and the oil measurement is lost forever.

8-11. Monitor Serial Signals

The serial signal is the last kind of signal that can be input to the RTU by a field device that we will discuss in this unit. Like most analog and pulse count inputs, a serial signal is sent to the RTU from an electronic processor of some kind. This will very often be a complex device such as an engine vibration analyzer or a process stream chromatograph. Usually, the signal or signals can be presented in the form of analog signals, but because the signals exist within the electronic processor as digital signals it is easier to move them as serial digital signals.

The physical connection used is often an RS-232 link, as shown in Figure 8-15. Acting as a master, the RTU signals the field device to respond; the device identifies itself and sends a serial message with a very fixed format, essentially telling the RTU all it knows. The RTU stores this data in registers as it comes in. When the MTU scans the RTU, the RTU includes this information with everything else it sends.

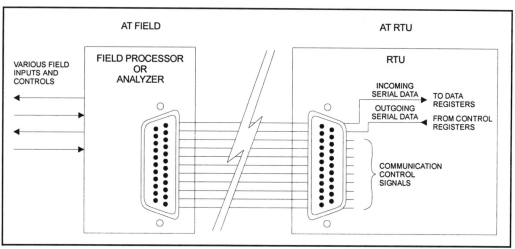

Figure 8-15. RS-232 Link

8-12. Non-RTU Functions

RTU functions are the functions that RTUs perform as RTUs. In addition, some RTUs that have computing capability can be programmed to perform other functions. Before deciding to program such RTUs to do other things, you should take care that you don't load too much onto the RTU. The potential concerns include overloading the CPU, exposing the equipment to electrical transients, exposing the software to people who are developing new programs, and meeting regulatory requirements involving the stability of data.

Exercises:

8-1.   *An RTU can gather data in the form of a discrete switch position. This is used for alarm and status monitoring. What three other forms of field data can an RTU gather?*

8-2.   *What four forms of signal can an RTU generate to control field equipment?*

8-3.   *What is the function of a protocol driver program?*

8-4.   *Many protocols divide the binary message into three fields. What are they?*

8-5.   *What is the purpose of the security code?*

8-6.   *Some protocols permit messages of differing lengths. How does the RTU know that it received all of the information?*

8-7.   *Why would you be unlikely to require sixteen bits in a register to define a valve position?*

8-8.   *Serial input to and output from RTUs is becoming more and more popular. Why?*

8-9.   *What is the purpose of a flow totalizer?*

Unit 9:
Master Terminal Units (MTUs)

UNIT 9

Master Terminal Units (MTUs)

At the center of each SCADA system is the device that issues all the commands, gathers all the data, stores some information, passes other information on to associated systems, interfaces with the people who operate the process, and actually seems to be in charge. This device is the master terminal unit (MTU). Some industries call it the "host computer."

Learning Objectives — When you have completed this unit, you should:

A. Understand what makes the MTU unique in a SCADA system.

B. Understand the main functions that an MTU performs.

C. Understand the concept of configuring as it applies to MTUs.

9-1. Communications Interface

The MTU must send information to each RTU. It almost always uses the same medium that the RTU uses to send information to it. It also uses the same protocol as the RTU. In these respects, the MTU has the same communications interface capabilities and equipment that we discussed in Unit 8 in connection with RTUs. The major difference is that, as a slave, the RTU cannot initiate a conversation; as a master, the MTU can. Its communications are initiated by programs within the MTU that can be triggered by manual instructions from the operator (very unusual) or by other programs within the MTU (normal method). More than 99 percent of all messages from the MTU to RTUs are automatically initiated.

The MTU must also communicate to the printers and CRTs that form the operator interface. It does this with techniques that are identical to those used by any computer. For this reason, these communications will not be covered in this book. Many MTUs are required to pass data upward to accounting computers, corporate business computers, or computer networks. In some cases, proprietary protocols will be used. In other cases, open products that are designed especially for intercomputer communications will be used. At this level of communication, peer-to-peer communication is more common than master-slave communication. Nearly all of this type of communication is handled by local area networks (LANs).

9-2. Configuring a Picture of the Process

For the MTU to do all of the things identified in the first paragraphs of this unit, a very detailed description of all of the sensors and actuators that are connected to the system must be available to the MTU's processor. To be handled in the most time-effective manner, this description must be arranged in a hierarchical form. Different hierarchical forms may benefit different processes, and frequently several possible paths through the process description will result in the same action. This statement will be explained in Example 9-1, on the closing of a pipeline block valve.

To visualize how the process picture can be described to the MTU, consider the very simple process shown in Figure 9-1, which represents a pipeline under the control of an MTU. At the input end of the pipeline, RTU number 1 monitors the status of a pump, which may be either on or off. It also allows the pump to be controlled, on or off, and a block valve to be controlled, open or closed, from the MTU. It monitors the position, open or closed, of the block valve and allows the accumulated flow or totalized flow of fluid going into the pipeline to be gathered from the MTU. Finally, RTU 1 provides for a low-pressure switch, which will be interpreted as an alarm, to be monitored from the MTU. At RTU 3, the same functions are available except that there is no pump to monitor or control. At RTU 2, there are only a block valve, which can be controlled and monitored, and the low-pressure alarm to be interfaced to the MTU. This is a very simple but workable SCADA system for monitoring and controlling a pipeline.

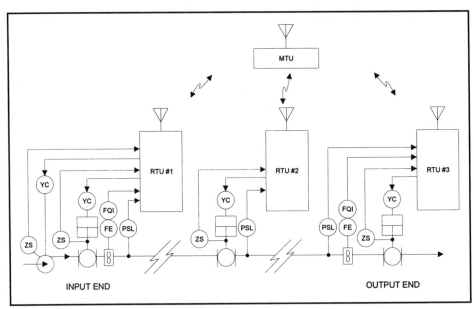

Figure 9-1. Pipeline under Control of a SCADA System

What this system is required to do is keep track of the fluid going into the pipeline on a twenty-four-hour basis, subtract the fluid going out of the pipeline, and create an alarm at the MTU so the operator will know when there is a problem. It should also watch the low-pressure alarm switches at each RTU and, if the pipeline is not working properly, create an alarm at the MTU. If the operator acts to shut in (turn off) the pipeline, the MTU should send a command on a high-priority basis to each RTU that has a block valve, ordering the RTU to close the block valve. At the same time, it should order RTU 1 to shut the pump. It should then check that each block valve closed. If the valve closed, the MTU should advise the operator. If the valve did not close, it should advise the operator and resend the command to the RTU, telling it again to close the valve. After some predetermined number of tries, the MTU should advise the operator that the valve refused to close and stop trying to close the valve.

In addition to these actions, which happen at shutdown, the MTU should inform the operator whenever it is asked of the status of the pump or block valves. The MTU should allow the operator to remotely open or close any one of the block valves. At shift changes and on request, it should print out a report that tells how much fluid was delivered out of the pipeline in the last shift, in the past twenty-four hours, and in the previous twenty-four-hour period. The MTU should also print, on a separate alarm printer, a description that includes the date and time of every change in an alarm condition as it occurs.

Later in this chapter we will look at some of the decisions the MTU must make to fulfill these requirements, but the purpose of this section is to understand how the process is described to the MTU. The process is called "configuring." It consists of filling in lookup tables that the MTU can use whenever it needs to know what its world looks like.

Many people are familiar with desktop computers that allow different screens or printers to be connected. When the computer is being set up, the operator will be asked questions about the make and model of the device that is connected to each of the computer's ports. By answering these questions, the operator is providing a picture of the process to the computer--or configuring the system. Thereafter, if the computer is required to output a message on LPT1, it will use the correct protocol at that port. Configuring an MTU is not much different, but there are many more questions to be answered.

On the physical level, as shown in Figure 9-2, configuring the MTU is very similar to configuring a desktop computer. A VDU or screen must be described (VGA, EGA, color, etc.), and the report printer must be described (protocol, paper feed, layout, etc.). The alarm log printer must be described in a similar way. The connections to the RTUs must be configured. Assuming full-duplex radio communications, the configuration information must include such things as the length of time it takes for the radio transmitter to turn on, the data rate, and the protocol. These describe the equipment that is physically connected to the MTU.

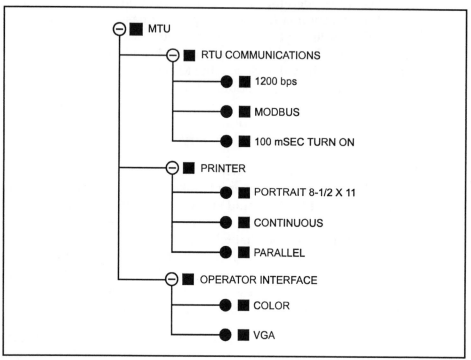

Figure 9-2. Configuring the MTU

Beyond the radio communication, more layers must be configured. The MTU must be told how many RTUs there are and what the identification of each of them is. In this example, Figure 9-3 shows that there are three RTUs and that their identification numbers are 1, 2, and 3. Written in binary, this would be 00000001, 00000010, and 00000011. The MTU must also know what is connected to each terminal at each RTU. The configuration of the MTU must, of course, be identical to the configuration of the RTU at this level. Only the RTU with identification number 1 will be considered here.

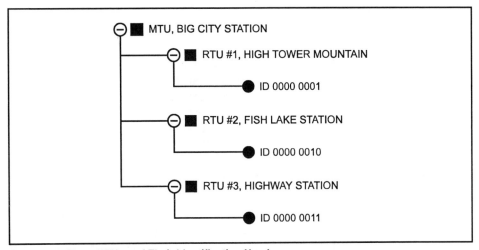

Figure 9-3. Three RTUs and Their Identification Numbers

In Figure 9-4, inputs to and outputs from the RTU have been grouped. At this stage we will be define all discrete outputs as being coded 001, all discrete inputs as 010, and all totalizer inputs as 011. If there were analog inputs, analog outputs, or pulse train outputs, they would also be identified as groups. Note that many of the configuration points within groups are shown as NC (not connected). RTUs are physically constructed as modular devices, and, even though only one totalizer is needed, the smallest module available may be four. The smallest module available for discrete outputs or discrete inputs may be four, eight, or sixteen. Figures 9-5 and 9-6 show samples of these modules.

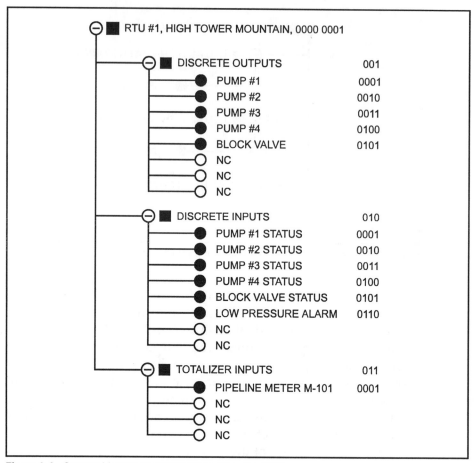

Figure 9-4. Grouped Inputs to and Outputs from the RTU

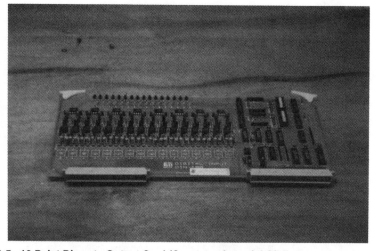

Figure 9-5. 16-Point Discrete Output Card (Courtesy: Imperial Oil Resources Ltd.)

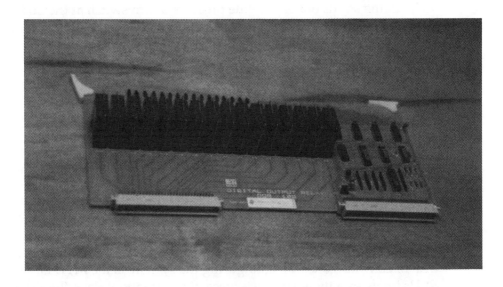

Figure 9-6. 16-Point Discrete Input Card (Courtesy: Imperial Oil Resources, Ltd.)

With this simple coding system, we have now described essentially
everything to which the MTU is connected. For example, to turn Pump
number 4 off, the MTU must deliver a signal to the modem that says, "Put
a 'zero' in the following register address":

RTU 1	0001	
Discrete Outputs	001	
Pump Number 4		0100

TOTAL ADDRESS   00010010100
TOTAL MESSAGE   000100101000

Similarly, to turn the pump on, the MTU must send a signal that says, "Put
a 'one' in the following register address":

RTU 1	0001	
Discrete Outputs	001	
Pump Number 4		0100

TOTAL ADDRESS   00010010100
TOTAL MESSAGE   000100101001

To learn the status of the low-line pressure alarm switch at the middle of the pipeline, the MTU must order RTU 2 to advise the status with the following code, which identifies a register position:

RTU 2	0010	
Discrete Input	010	
Position 5		0101

TOTAL MESSAGE   00100100101

Depending on whether a zero or a one is in this register position, the MTU will infer that the pressure is high or normal.

Notice that one bit, the smallest available quantum of data, is sufficient to change a valve position or to read a status switch. However, this is true only if a great deal of planning has gone into the message and if a great deal of care has gone into configuring the system so the MTU and the RTUs know exactly where each piece of information exists. Totalizer inputs and analog points are slightly more complex than discrete points. The information in these signal types cannot be contained in one bit.

Usually, an analog or totalizer word consists of sixteen bits (although it may be eight, twelve, or thirty-two). As long as both the MTU and RTU are configured the same and the communications protocol can handle the word size, the number of bits doesn't matter. The message sent by the MTU to the RTU will describe the register location of the first bit of the word. When the RTU gets this message, it will send the information that is in that location as well as the following fifteen locations to the MTU.

With this amount of detail, the MTU can be advised of what is happening everywhere in its universe. It can also reach every point that is connected to it to effect changes. Some clarification is still required. It would be a real nuisance if the operator had to memorize these long codes, which are so easy for a computer to manipulate. An operator input-output interface or human-machine interface must be configured. After it has, when the operator asks about the low-pressure alarm condition at RTU 1, the MTU will know that it is being asked what bit is in register position 0100101 in RTU number 0001; it will know that if it finds a one in that register position, the message it should send to the VDU is "Pipeline inlet pressure is normal."

When all this configuring has been done, the SCADA system has a complete picture of the process and has the ability to communicate this information to the operators, RTUs, and others.

9-3.   Some Simple Applications

Until an application is defined to the MTU, a picture of the process will be useless. Many standard applications apply to most SCADA systems. For example, one application might require that the MTU start a scan of every RTU every ten minutes. Another application might require that the condition of every alarm point that is read be compared to its condition or to the previous scan and that, if there is a difference, the new condition plus the time of the last scan be printed on the alarm log.

These simple modular applications, which the MTU can treat as subroutines, can be combined with one another into useful, more complex applications. In programming parlance, they are equipped with "hooks" that allow them to be connected together.

Example 9-1. Using the SCADA layout and configuration defined earlier in this unit, let's investigate a leak detection application. Several better ways to detect leaks exist, but this method has been used successfully and has the attraction of being simple. It is called the volume balance method.

The principle of this method is that for a noncompressible fluid (liquid) pipeline, what goes in should equal what goes out. If the flow rate out of the pipe is greater than the flow rate into the pipe, there is a measurement error, and perhaps one or more of the meters need recalibration. If the output is less than the input, there are two possibilities: a measurement error or another undesirable output from the pipeline--a leak. The dynamics of the pipeline, particularly volume changes due to pressure surges, may cause short-term inequalities that can be filtered out by comparing running average inputs and outputs.

The layout of the application will look like this:

1.   Conduct a scan of each RTU every ten minutes (scan).

2.   Add the new line input meter reading to the previous four line input meter readings and divide by five (running average filter of input).

3.   Add the new line output meter reading to the previous four line output meter readings and divide by five (running average filter of output).

4.   Subtract the sum of line output meter readings from the sum of line input meter readings (difference).

5.   Divide the difference obtained in step 4 by the sum obtained in step 2 (error ratio).

6. Multiply the product obtained in step 5 by 100 (percentage error per scan).

7. Compare the number from step 6 to a number selected by the operator and defined as the "minimum error for alarm."

8. If the percentage of error is less than this operator-selected number, no further action is required. Go back to step 1.

9. If the percentage of error is greater than this operator-selected number, check that an alarm was generated on the previous scan. If so, no further action is required. Go back to step 1. If the number from step 6 is negative, send an alarm to the VDU that says, "Meter error in input meter or output meter! Check calibration." Send the same message with the time stamp to the alarm log. Go back to step 1.

10. If the number from step 6 is positive, send an alarm to the VDU that says, "Potential pipeline leak." Send the same message with the time stamp to the alarm log. Go back to step 1.

Several changes could be made to this application to make it more useful, and many details would need to be added to make the application really work, but enough detail was shown in Example 9-1 to give you an idea of how an application works.

Example 9-2. One of the economic benefits of a SCADA system is that it enables an operator to make routine, manually initiated, remote control changes. In this example, we will rough out an application that allows the block valve at the pipeline inlet to be closed. The layout of the application will look like this:

1. If a keyboard entry calling for "Close pipeline inlet block valve" is made, set a flag (put a 1) in the MTU register reserved for this function.

2. Each time a scan is ordered, check this MTU register and compare what is in it to a register in the MTU that tells what the status of that valve is (1 for closed, 0 for open).

3. If the registers are the same, send a message to the VDU that says, "Pipeline inlet block valve is already closed." Go to standby mode.

4. If the registers are different, include an order in this scan that tells the block valve at RTU 1 to close.

5.   After the next scan, check that the block valve status at RTU 1 reads "closed." If it does, send a message to the VDU that says, "Pipeline inlet block valve is now closed." Go to standby mode.

6.   If the status reads "open," resend the control order on the following scan.

7.   After one more scan, check that the valve closed. If it did, send a message to the VDU that says, "Pipeline inlet block valve is now closed." Go to standby mode.

8.   If the valve is still not closed, send a message to the VDU and to the alarm printer that says, "Pipeline inlet block valve refuses to close." Go to standby mode.

Example 9-3. You can see that when the SCADA system has determined that there is a "potential pipeline leak" the operator may want to move quickly to close all block valves. Rather than calling for a series of individual applications, each one of which will close and verify one block valve, another application can be developed. The layout of the application could look like this:

1.   If a keyboard entry calling for "Shut in the pipeline" is made, set a flag (put a 1) in the MTU register reserved for closing pipeline block valve at RTU 1, turning the pump off at RTU 1, closing the pipeline block valve at RTU 2, and closing the pipeline block valve at RTU 3.

Each one of the four individual instructions should be completed with the same amount of detail as shown in Example 9-2.

2.   Instead of waiting for the next regular scan, this order to "Shut in the pipeline" has a sufficiently high priority to initiate a special scan to these RTUs that are involved in shutting in the line.

3.   After ordering the RTUs, the MTU should go back to each of them to check for compliance. After advising the operator that the pipeline is shut in, the MTU should return to regular scan.

More and more complex applications can be built up using simpler applications as modules or subroutines.

9-4.   Data Storage

In the same way that the RTU is required to store certain critical pieces of data, such as meter values, for extended periods of time, MTUs must retain certain classes of data. Their ability to pass information to the next higher level computer may be inhibited by the failure of machine-to-machine connections. An estimate of the longest time needed to discover and repair such a failure, including an adequate safety margin, should form a basis for calculating how much of the history of these critical data sets must be retained.

Before the capabilities of graphical interface tools existed, there was not much incentive to store large amounts of data. SCADA is an operating tool, so references to what happened four months ago was not seen as being very useful to operators. When graphical tools like trending became available, this situation changed. Operators could call on a trend of nearly any data point plotted against time. Plotting two or more trends provided information about the interdependence of sets of data that was otherwise difficult to visualize. This created demand for MTUs equipped with larger data historians.

The pendulum is swinging in the other direction now that computers have high-speed access to other databases via network communications. Figure 9-7 shows a block diagram of a system that allows an MTU, as well as many other subsystems, to store some of its data in a central data store. This capability will cause most of the data that is not critical for the operation (such as historian information) to be stored in the central data store. The data that is vital, such as lookup tables and configuration information, will continue to be stored in the MTU.

Much of the information needed to operate the SCADA system is of no interest to others outside SCADA. It is probably not worth retaining and will be erased after an expiration date is reached.

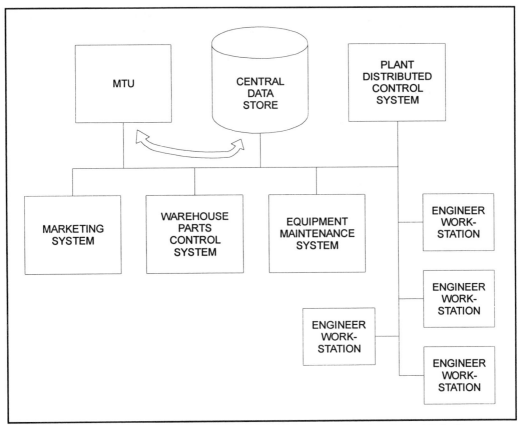

Figure 9-7. Block Diagram of a System That Allows an MTU to Store Data in a Central Data Store

Exercises:

9-1.   *An MTU is the only station that can initiate a conversation with another station. This statement describes what kinds of communication?*

9-2.   *Only one station has a definition of the entire process in its memory. What is this called?*

9-3.   *Each RTU has a part of that definition. What defines those things that the RTU must know about?*

9-4.   *MTUs communicate to three classes of machines. What are they?*

9-5.   *By using groups of simple applications, the MTU can accomplish more complex applications. Examples 9-2 and 9-3 in this unit illustrated this for a pipeline and its block valves, respectively. Develop a similar scenario for an electric power transmission scheme in which the MTU has the ability to interrupt certain loads when demand for power is high.*

9-6.   Inexpensive memory has led more and more information to be stored in the MTU. What technology may turn that trend around? Why?

9-7.   What effect do graphics have on memory demand?

9-8.   In addition to communicating with other machines, storing information, and interfacing with the operator, what does the MTU do?

Unit 10: Sensors, Actuators, and Wiring

UNIT 10

Sensors, Actuators, and Wiring

The details of any project can easily be overshadowed by its one or two most prominent or obvious highlights. With SCADA projects, for example, the features that attract the eye are the MTU, the communications system, or the RTUs. It may therefore come as a surprise to learn that such apparently simple and inexpensive parts as limit switches, valve actuators, and equipment analyzers usually represent the largest portion of the capital cost of a SCADA project. This is particularly true if the project involves the modification of an existing process so it interfaces with SCADA.

Learning Objectives — When you have completed this unit, you should:

A. Be aware that the cost of process interface equipment can be significant.

B. Recognize that when sensors and actuators are being selected and installed the special considerations of the process and ambient conditions must be taken into account.

10-1. A Forgotten Cost

This chapter—indeed, this entire Independent Learning Module—will make no attempt to discuss all of the types of sensors and actuators that SCADA systems can use to interface with the processes that they control and monitor. Several sensors and actuators will be discussed as examples, but it should be obvious by now that many industries use SCADA. Each of those industries has many measurement and control requirements that are unique. However, most of these requirements can be handled in several ways by many different pieces of equipment. Multiplying "many" by "many" by "several" by "many" culminates in a very large result indeed. For most SCADA RTU locations, this same kind of vast arithmetic can be applied to calculating the cost of the sensors and actuators associated with SCADA.

Rightly or wrongly, the economics of establishing an RTU at a particular location is usually based on taking one or two valuable measurements remotely and making one, two, or sometimes three changes remotely or automatically from a distant control location. It is on these three or four functional benefits that the cost of the installation must be justified. As soon as the feasibility of installation for these three or four functions is established, the phase "Wouldn't it be nice if ..." rises to the top of the hit parade. The hurdle has been cleared; the MTU and the RTU have been justified. So everything else is free, right?

What is forgotten by the uninitiated is that the sensors, the actuators, and the wiring between them and the RTU also cost money. In fact, these items frequently cost three to four times more than the RTU, UPS, and communications equipment at a particular site. Figure 10-1 shows the costs of SCADA at a simple RTU site. In the figure, there is only one RTU, one radio, and one power supply at a remote site. However, that site may easily have as many as 250 sensors, actuators, and analyzers.

Item	Cost
RTU cost (includes panel)	6,900
Radio System (includes path study)	1,150
Uninterruptible Power Supply (24 VDC)	2,000
Instrumentation	
Sensors	9,200
Actuators	8,625
Heater Automatic/Remote Ignitor	3,450
Installation/Wiring of Instrumentation	5,000
Engineering	
Design, Configuration, Procurement	10,000
Drafting	4,000
Total Cost	**50,325**

Figure 10-1. The Costs of SCADA at Simple RTU Site (Courtesy of Tartan Engineering Corp. Ltd.)

Many of the things an operator does while visiting a remote site are done automatically. He or she does them by using the enormously versatile sensing and actuating capabilities of the human body. We have been augmenting these capabilities for the past sixty-four million years, ever since the world's population of dinosaurs moved over to make room for mammals. Since 1769, when James Watt developed improvements to the steam engine and the Industrial Revolution began, we have been recognizing parameters that need to be measured and controls that need to be adjusted. Generally speaking, we are very well matched to the measurement and control functions that process operators are required to fulfill because those functions have been established with operators in mind.

Specialized tools have developed as industry has grown. When it became important to know not just whether a liquid was "hot" or "cold" thermometers were developed. When enough people had to know the height of liquid in a vessel, sensors that a person could read were built, even when the atmosphere above the liquid was 500°F at a pressure of six atmospheres and consisted of combustible, carcinogenic vapors.

The point is that many years of engineering effort have been invested perfecting sensors and actuators so a person-operator can interface with the process. When a SCADA system is installed between the operator and the process, some additional engineering effort is required. For example, the patent has run out on the thermometer, but it may not have run out on the noncontact, infrared-sensing, 4-20 mA output thermal-imaging device. The patent has run out on the quarter-turn, hand-operated ball valve actuator, but it may not have run out on the pneumatically controlled, Scotch yoke, spring-opposed, fail-safe ball valve actuator.

Sensors that are cheap to buy if they are to be read by a human operator are usually more expensive if they are to be read by a machine. The thermometer to be fitted into a thermowell in a process vessel (shown in Figure 10-2) will cost about $50. However, a temperature transmitter to be fitted into the same thermowell and to output a 4-20 mA signal into an RTU (shown in Figure 10-3) will cost $600. The ratio of costs for the local versus the remote measurement of pressure or level is similar.

Figure 10-2. Thermometer to Fit into Thermowell in a Process Vessel

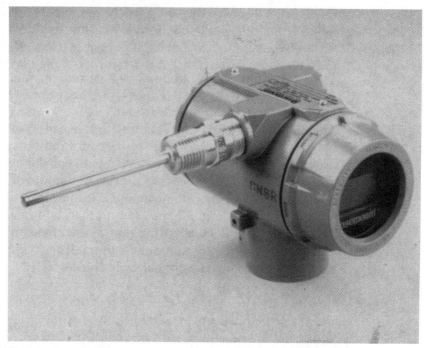

Figure 10-3. Temperature Transmitter (Courtesy: Rosemount Instruments, Ltd.)

Besides purchase cost, there is a cost associated with connecting the sensor or actuator to the RTU. Copper wire is normally used because the signals are normally low-voltage electrical. In many applications, shielding must be added over the copper wire to prevent electromagnetic interference or noise from corrupting the signal. Some form of physical protection of the copper wire and shield is necessary; it may take the form of some type of flexible armor that is integral to the structure of the cable. It may be that the unarmored cable is fed through rigid pipes called conduit or laid in protective channels called cable tray. Finally, the cable is encapsulated in a jacket of fluid-proof, flexible plastic. One reason for this is to prevent moisture or corrosive atmospheres from reaching the conductors and shields. The other reason is to prevent toxic or flammable fluids from traveling through the cable from the process areas to areas that are normally free of these fluids.

Figure 10-4 shows a cutaway drawing of such a cable. Many pairs of copper wires, each capable of carrying the signal from one sensor or to one actuator, can be integrated into a cable. Process instruments are not large enough to allow multipair cables to enter their wiring box, pass through, and carry on to the next instrument; junction boxes or field termination boxes are used to overcome this. Figure 10-5 shows a large multipair cable coming from an RTU to a concentration of instruments, in this case status switches on ball valves. At a convenient location near the concentration, a junction box (Figure 10-6) with terminal strips is mounted. The wires from the multipair cable are terminated in the junction box. Smaller cables, often with only one or two pairs of wires, are run from this junction box to the individual instruments.

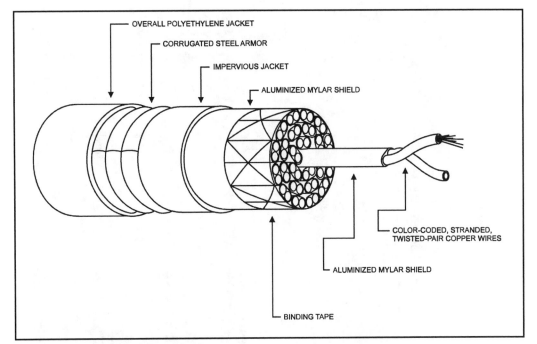

Figure 10-4. Cutaway Drawing of Cable

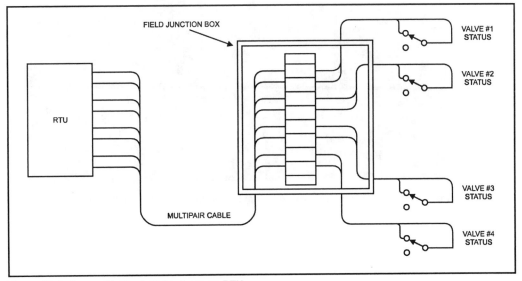

Figure 10-5. Large, Multipair Cable from an RTU

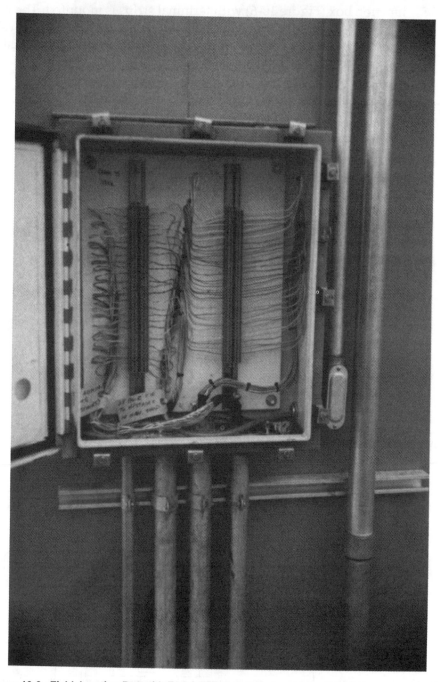

Figure 10-6. Field Junction Box with Terminal Strips (Courtesy: Imperial Oil Resources, Ltd.)

The physical configuration of the process may mean that several of these multipair cables will need to connect to the RTU. Often when this is done a large junction box, called a marshaling panel, is located at the RTU location (see Figure 10-7). Terminal strips in this box allow all the wiring to the process instruments to be wired and checked for correctness before the RTU is even delivered to the construction site. The marshaling panel also acts as the platform for power relays, control power fuses or circuit breakers, intrinsically safe barriers, and special calibration or testing circuitry. If small numbers of special instruments are required, such as flowmeter totalizers, pollution-monitoring electronics, or process moisture analyzers, they are often housed in the marshaling panel. Very often, the marshaling panel even houses a few status lights and manual controls. If local, manually read meter outputs are mandated, they also are usually located here. Figure 10-8 shows the front of the marshaling panel.

Figure 10-7. Marshaling Panel—RTU in Lower Center (Courtesy: Imperial Oil Resources, Ltd.)

Figure 10-8. Front View of RTU Marshaling Panel (Courtesy: Imperial Oil Resources, Ltd.)

All of this technical equipment must be specified. Installation drawings and instructions must be developed. Documentation of the system, individual equipment, licenses, software, and operating instructions must be gathered or written. In short, the engineering of the SCADA field installation must be performed.

Because of the high relative complexity of a SCADA system, the ratio of engineering cost to total project cost may often be three to five times as high as would be expected for a non-SCADA project. Engineering, development, and documentation costs may reach 50 percent of the total SCADA project cost compared to 10 percent to 15 percent of the cost of nonautomated process projects.

10-2. Special Considerations

Each industry has process considerations that make it if not unique then certainly distinct. Production processing and the transportation of hydrocarbon fluids require that the sensors, actuators, and wiring used in these processes not initiate fires and explosions. Chemical processing may face these same issues, but it will also be concerned with corrosion caused by the process fluids and the pollution of the surrounding atmosphere. Electric power generation and transmission must deal with the issue of isolating instruments from strong electrical fields and high voltages. Food processing has to be concerned that field equipment that comes into contact with the food will not contaminate it. Each of these special considerations can be met by existing equipment if there is enough of a market for the equipment and if the purchasers are prepared to pay enough. But there will be an extra charge.

As an example, Figure 10-9 shows how a simple device (a cam-operated limit switch) operates. On the left side of the figure, a simple form C, single-pole, double-throw switch is equipped with a lever that is moved by a cam on a valve shaft. When the shaft moves down, contacts "com" and "no" close, indicating that the valve is closed. In a clean, noncombustible atmosphere, the housing for this switch can be designed so support for the working parts is the primary consideration. The materials used can be low-cost cast plastic. The cost will be about $20.

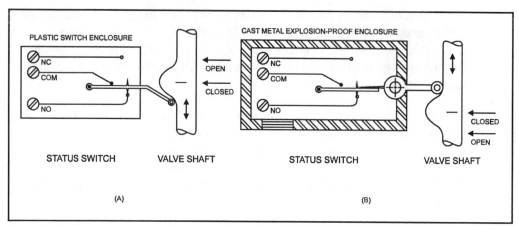

Figure 10-9. How a Cam-operated Limit Switch Operates

The right side of Figure 10-9 shows a switch that functions the same way as the switch shown on the left side of the figure. The atmosphere in this case is often 20 percent methane. A common way to address this condition is to design an explosion-proof housing for the switch. The housing is not designed to keep the atmosphere away from the contacts; it is designed to be so strong that if a combustible atmosphere does exist and the switch contacts ignite the atmosphere inside, the housing will not break up and explode. In addition, the clearance between the moving and mating surfaces (the lever shaft and the housing cover) must be tight enough to allow the expanding gases to escape and must be long enough to cool them so they do not ignite the atmosphere when they do escape. The materials for this enclosure will be metal, and the surfaces will be machined. The cost will be about $400.

10-3. Standardization

Very few sensors and actuators are so unusual that they are made by only one manufacturer. As market conditions change, the prices of one manufacturer's product relative to another's will vary, and there may be a temptation to shift from one supplier of the process end devices to another. This temptation should be resisted. Changing suppliers because the product is of inferior quality or because it is no longer available is acceptable. But small price savings can easily be overshadowed by the increased costs of warehousing, training personnel, the time lost replacing the old product, changes to drawings and other documentation, and calibration procedures. If the SCADA system will be installed in an existing facility, you should consult local maintenance personnel to learn which suppliers have provided good service in the past.

A survey should be made of potential suppliers of sensors and actuators early in the planning stages of a SCADA system. In addition to the fitness of the manufacturer's sensors and actuators to the purposes of the device, consideration should be given to the financial stability of the manufacturer and the manufacturer's history of supporting equipment that is no longer marketed. Ideally, spares for each part that forms your SCADA system will be available until you decommission it. However, an acceptable second-best situation might be that replacement parts for the sensors and actuators will continue to be available for at least ten years after they cease to be marketed.

The reason that this is more important for sensors and actuators than for MTUs and RTUs is that MTUs and RTUs do not have very many moving parts. They may suffer from a lot of failures when they are first installed (so-called infant mortality) but, unless subjected to long-term overheating, they can be expected to run without trouble for a long time afterward. On the other hand, sensors and actuators do have moving parts that wear out. They are exposed to process chemicals, shifts in ambient temperature, vibration, and a host of other conditions that contribute to failure. The planning for a SCADA project should include provision for maintenance, and those maintenance plans should concentrate on sensors and actuators.

10-4. Maintenance

The maintenance requirements in a SCADA system are not significantly different than those in most other high-technology control systems. However, the communications equipment, radios, modems, and protocol drivers are the exception. The calibration, validation, and servicing of these devices will require special equipment and manpower training that is not generally available. Depending on the size of your SCADA system and the availability of contract service companies with these particular talents and resources, you may have to make sure your company provides for this maintenance.

When you are establishing the proper level of service for your SCADA system you should do it with the expectation that requirements will be high initially and then will drop off to a lower plateau (see Figure 10-10). As noted earlier in this unit, the maintenance requirements of the sensors and actuators will have different profiles. There will be a high initial maintenance level as new equipment goes through its early mortality stage and as loose contacts and pinched wires from the manufacturing and construction phases make themselves known. But after this early phase is over, the process interface devices will continue to wear and fail at a higher rate than will the solid-state equipment (see Figure 10-11). To anticipate this, the facility's design should allow for ease of access, temporary isolation from the process, and manual monitoring and control while the sensors and actuators are being calibrated or replaced.

This unit has concentrated on some of the considerations to be kept in mind when using sensors and actuators. As used in SCADA, these devices may not be significantly different from the instruments that fulfill similar functions in a highly automated plant in a similar industry. However, they will be different from instruments that are designed to be read directly by a human operator. SCADA sensors and actuators tend to be expensive to buy and maintain, a fact that should be taken into account when you develop cost estimates for SCADA installations.

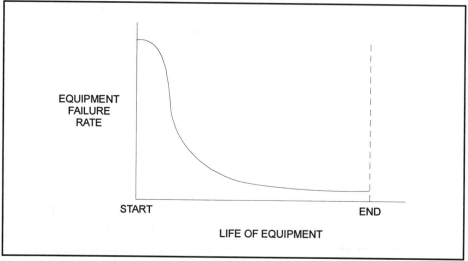

Figure 10-10. Failure Profile of Solid-State Equipment

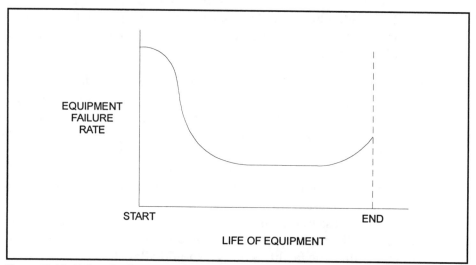

Figure 10-11. Failure Profile of Mechanical Equipment

Exercises:

10-1. *Why will a patent on a measurement device likely increase its cost?*

10-2. *Why is electric wire the most common medium for moving signals between the RTU and the field devices?*

10-3. *What special feature of oil and gas processing increases the cost of many of the sensors used in those industries?*

10-4. *What is the primary purpose of a marshaling panel? Name three other purposes.*

10-5. *What are field termination boxes used for?*

10-6. *Why are engineering charges higher for SCADA than for most other projects?*

10-7. *Name four factors that would increase the cost of a project if the same type of sensor were purchased from multiple manufacturers.*

10-8. *Why do maintenance costs peak at the beginning of a SCADA project?*

Unit 11: Applications

UNIT 11

Applications

No accumulation of parts or subsystems can be justified unless it serves some useful purpose. This unit will discuss some of the common purposes or applications that SCADA systems are built for. Perhaps more importantly, it will also present features of SCADA systems that contribute to the practicality of applications so you may evaluate your own applications.

Learning Objectives — When you have completed this unit, you should:

A.   Be aware of the broad classes of applications to which SCADA is applied.

B.   Recognize those features that support and those that inhibit the application of SCADA.

11-1. Real Time Revisited

As we learned in Unit 4, the time lag associated with transferring information from a field sensor to the RTU (or from the RTU to a field-mounted actuator) is essentially zero. RTU scan rates are fast. On the other hand, significant time delays are caused by low communication data rates and protocols that encourage regular, scheduled interrogation of each point in the system by the MTU. The time delay required to correct a problem may be as much as two scan periods. See Figure 11-1 for an application that involves the MTU. This inherent potential time delay is not critical for many applications, but for others it can be the determining factor. Some applications simply will not work when a significant time delay is introduced.

In Figure 11-1, a SCADA system monitors the operation of a bank of compressors and a distribution pipeline to learn if the compressors are running and to keep track of the pressure of gas in the line. The gas is injected at specific points into oil wells, and the resultant reduction in average density of the well-bore fluid causes more oil per hour to get to the surface. Each well has a different productivity of oil raised per unit of gas injected. If some of the compressors fail and the pressure of the distribution system starts to drop some wells will stop producing. These gas-lift systems may be large, covering hundreds of square miles. Restarting a gas-lift well usually requires that an operator visit each well, often for several hours, until it stabilizes. The incentive for optimizing the wells that are shut in, or turned off, can be great. It may be that the lowest-productivity wells or the wells located closest to the operations center are shut in first.

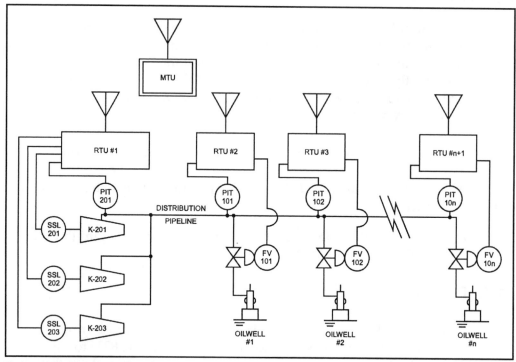

Figure 11-1. SCADA Monitoring and Controlling a Gas Lift System

The pipeline has enough capacity to maintain a working pressure for about ten or fifteen minutes before wells randomly stop producing. In Figure 11-1, the MTU scans each RTU every five minutes. In the worst case, the compressor fails just after its RTU is scanned (see Figure 11-2). The RTU at the compressor site learns of the failure quickly, in about one second, but must wait until the next scan, which occurs five minutes later, to pass the data to the MTU. In less than one second after it learned of the compressor failure, the MTU has applied an algorithm to the data and has decided which wells should be shut in. It can now start sending instructions to selected wells to turn off, but at this scan rate it will be another five minutes before the last RTU (and well) has received its instructions. Process calculations can be performed, or actual measurements taken, to determine if this response is fast enough. If necessary, such special provisions as scanning the compressor RTU two times in each regular scan may gain the couple of minutes of response that will make the difference between a workable and a nonworkable system. This application would work within the constraints of scan times.

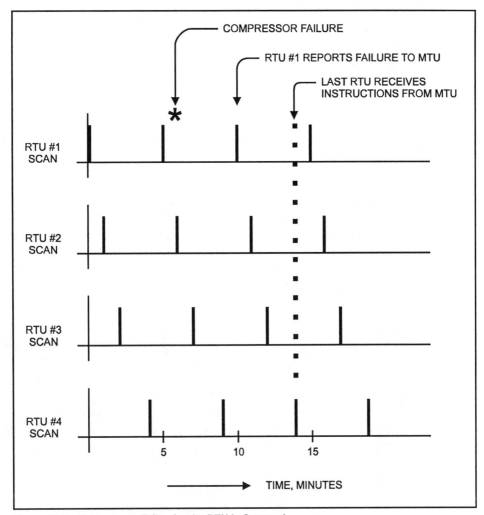

Figure 11-2. Compressor Fails after Its RTU Is Scanned

On the other hand, an application for generating electricity and performing transmission load-shedding, which is closely analogous to the application just described, would almost certainly not work with the communication speeds described. Permissible scan times on the order of seconds would be required. Constraints like these determine system specifications. In fact, many SCADA systems used by electric utilities provide scan times of one to five seconds.

11-2. Accounting and Grade of Data

The custody transfer of a commodity requires the seller and buyer to mutually agree on several points. These points are usually listed in an agreement—a contract—between the two parties. One of the important points of a contract is the price that will be paid for each unit of the commodity. Another is the number of units that are transferred. When one of the parties, usually the buyer, is a member of the public or is otherwise considered to be potentially incapable of protecting itself in the exchange, a regulatory agency may become involved. As a result, we have residential electricity meters that have been calibrated under the authority of a regulatory agency and have been mechanically sealed (see Figure 11-3) to prevent tampering. Gasoline pumps are calibrated and sealed in a similar fashion.

The transfer of ownership of many industrial commodities occurs at remote locations. Methane moving from a gas transmission pipeline to a city distribution system may be metered fifteen kilometers from the city. Irrigation water may be metered where the aqueduct crosses a state line. Electric power sold from one utility company to another may be metered at the boundary between the two utility jurisdictions. The unit cost of the commodities is not an issue when SCADA is used for custody transfer.

Figure 11-3. Mechanically Sealed Residential Electrical Meters

Using SCADA to ascertain the number of units transferred does raise two issues, that is, the accuracy and the security of the measurement. Accuracy is usually the lesser concern. Most measurements used in custody transfer start by gauging a simple parameter and then adjust it by applying fixed and variable correction factors. For some measurements, there are few corrections, and their effects are not large. Other measurements require that ten or more parameters be input to an algorithm to generate the custody transfer amount. Figure 11-4 shows an example in which gas volumes are measured by measuring the pressure drop across the orifice (the static pressure and temperature may also be measured). In addition, information about the size of the pipe and the orifice, the density and composition of the gas, and several other things may be included in the calculation. To achieve acceptable accuracy, all of these corrections must be made. If the algorithm to incorporate all of the corrections is to be run at the measurement point, additional computing power will have to be purchased, installed, and maintained at each measurement point. It would make better financial sense to share the computing power among several metering points and gather the totalized meter reading for each meter point. This is very often done, and, in fact, manufacturers of orifice meter totalizers usually offer a model that can provide this capability for three or more meter runs (see Figure 11-5).

$$Q_v = F_b \, F_r \, Y \, F_{pb} \, F_{tb} \, F_{tf} \, F_{gr} \, F_{pv} \, (h_w \, P_{f1})^{0.5}$$

where:

F_b = a function of the orifice and meter tube diameter
F_r = a function of the fluid Reynolds number
Y = a function of the compressibility of the fluid
F_{pb} = a function of the legal contract base pressure
F_{tb} = a function of the legal contract base temperature
F_{tf} = a function of the actual fluid temperature
F_{gr} = a function of the fluid density
F_{pv} = a function of the compressibility of the fluid
h_w = the differential pressure across the orifice
P_{f1} = the static pressure at the orifice plate

Figure 11-4. Gas Volumes Measured by Measuring Pressure Drop across the Orifice

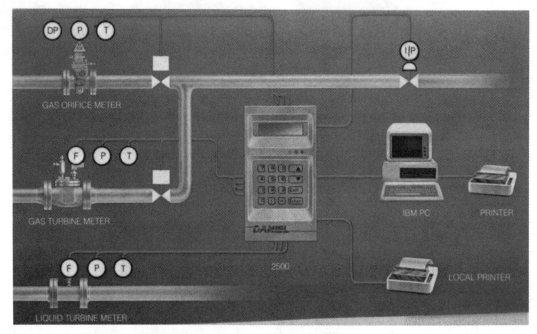

Figure 11-5. Totalizer for Multiple Meters (Courtesy: Daniel Industries Inc.)

The ultimate extension of this philosophy would be to bring the variable parameter or parameters associated with each metered stream all the way back to the MTU and do the computing there. In earlier systems where this was done the computing load this placed on the MTU was severe enough to degrade the overall system. Faster computers may have overcome this problem, but there is a more basic reason for not doing the calculations at the MTU. Many of the basic measurement parameters must be integrated over time to arrive at a useful accounting value. In the case of the previous example of an orifice meter, the basic parameter measured is differential pressure, which is related to flow rate. To get to the accounting units, which are likely to be mass or volume, it is necessary to integrate individual flow rate readings over time. The more often the flow rates are read and integrated, the more accurate the result will be. Scan rates from MTUs are often too infrequent to produce an acceptable accuracy level. Failures of the communications system or of other equipment would further degrade the accuracy.

If the MTU scan rate and the unreliability of the communications system preclude doing the computation there, how about doing it in the RTU? Some systems do use the RTU to calculate accounting- grade information. Most modern RTUs offer the ability to program in one or more higher-level computer languages, so the capability to do the calculations is there. The RTU does scan its inputs frequently enough for most measurement requirements and can handle the computation load associated with a few meter points. Before using the RTU as a totalizer, you should take into account the maintenance of the meter totalizing function. Built-for-purpose totalizers usually make it easy for a qualified person to change algorithm variables through push-button control. To make the same change in an RTU program may require burning in an EPROM (erasable programmable read-only memory).

Security is at least as important as accuracy when handling custody transfer information. The wire and lead seals used on mechanical meters are there to show whether the meter factor was tampered with after it was officially calibrated. In some cases, this technique has carried over to the present. Meter totalizers are sometimes required to be enclosed in tamper-proof boxes, complete with wire and tab seals.

In other cases, a software security code known by only a restricted number of people must form part of the access procedure for changing totalizing algorithm variables. In some cases, a hard copy must be printed at stated time intervals to establish to the accounting department's satisfaction what these variables were. Figure 11-6 is an example of such a hard-copy printout. In many cases, the current totalized flow must be visually confirmable by an inspector at all times. Even with our current ability to move complex data electronically, the need for a "paper trail" is still with us. This does not mean, however, that the regular billing will wait for a manual confirmation. Most often, the billing is done on the basis of the electronically gathered data. Auditing is usually done on a nonperiodic basis to confirm that the electronically gathered billing information is correct.

Meter Log Record

Date: 96.08.15

Tag Number: FT_702, PT_702, TT_702

Description: Dry gas to injection.

Physical Data:
Orifice Size: 101.60 mm   Pipe Diameter: 202.4 mm

Base Conditions:
PB =   101.325 kPag   TB =   15.00 C

Local Barometric Pressure = 100.00 kPa

Calibration:
FT_702   0-25.0 kPa
PT_702   0-689.5 kPag
TT_702   5-39.0 C

Operating Average: (24 hr)
FT_702   15.0 kPa
PT_702   450.0 kPag
TT_702   25.0 C

CPRIME: (24 hr average)
Fb   3369.42
Fr   1.0004
Y   1.0046
Fpb   1.0023
Ftf   0.9881
Fgr   1.0541
Fpv   1.0081
Fa   1.0000

Total Flow: (24 hr average)
FQI_702 = 166.617 km^3/d

Figure 11-6. Hard-Copy Printout (Courtesy of Crystal Engineering Ltd.)

11-3. Scanning and Communications

The applications concerned with scanning and communications are put in place to monitor and, in some cases, to modify or correct problems associated with these two functions. The scanning of the various RTUs by the MTU is itself an application. A relatively simple program runs so as to define the order in which the RTUs will be scanned. This order is usually adjustable or configurable by the SCADA system operator to optimize the operation of the process. Consider a system (see Figure 11-7) that includes a pipeline that carries incompressible fluids and has one meter point measuring fluid into the line and six meter points measuring fluid out of the line. The algorithm would be "Subtract all output meter readings from all input meter readings and alarm if the difference exceeds 5 percent of the input."

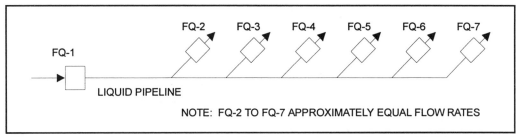

Figure 11-7. Pipeline for Incompressible Fluids That Has Meter Points for Measuring Fluid into and out of the Line

What is not stated in this algorithm is that the readings should all be taken at the same time. In fact, if the scan period for this system were long and the meters were read at other than the optimal times, a systematic error would be introduced (see Figure 11-8). That error could be reduced, probably to the point of inconsequentiality, by arranging to read half of the outputs, then the input, then the other half of the outputs. A slightly different and more effective strategy, shown in Figure 11-9, would be to scan those RTUs that contributed one half of the pipeline output, followed by the RTU that provided the pipeline input, followed in turn by the RTUs that provided the other half of the pipeline output. The scanning application would have to be modified if additional pipeline outputs were added after the system was initially built.

Different types of scans may be needed depending on the process situation. When everything is normal, the best scan is likely to be one that interrogates and provides instructions to an RTU and then waits for a response before moving to the next RTU. In an upset condition where it is very important that the correct control actions occur, the best scan would be one that involves having each RTU confirm that it received the correct message before the RTU acts on the message. In an upset situation where the speed of the actuator's response becomes more important, a more effective scan may be one that sends out a single instruction to each RTU in rapid succession without waiting for a response.

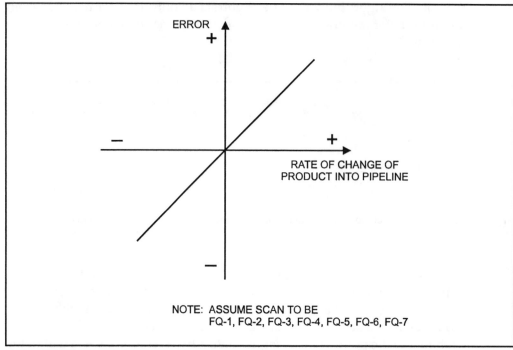

Figure 11-8. Systematic Error Introduced by Long Scan Period and Nonoptimal Meter Reading Times

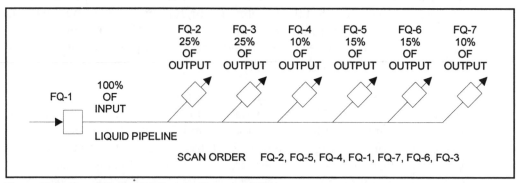

Figure 11-9. More Effective Strategy for Scanning RTUs

Communications-related applications are frequently used to keep track of failures to communicate and to alert the operator, either by a daily report or by an audible or visual alarm, when the ratio of unsuccessful communication attempts to successful ones exceeds some value. That value is selectable by the operator. As we learned earlier, a message put together by an MTU will include the identification of the RTU to which it is sent as well as a message and an error-detection code. For most classes of message, the RTU is expected to respond to the MTU by indicating that it received the message. If the MTU does not receive the response, it will consider this communication attempt to be a failure. It will add one failure to the total number of failures for that RTU, and it will resend the message. After a preselectable number of consecutive failures to one RTU, it will move on to the next RTU in the scan sequence. Usually, the simple failure of one random message will do nothing except appear on a daily communication failure report. The failure of three or four consecutive communication attempts to an RTU will probably trigger an alarm to the system operator that maintenance is required on that communication circuit.

An inspection of the daily communication report can often point to circuits that are becoming marginal. Responding to the information in these reports allows many problems to be corrected before they cause lost production or increased operating cost. A second communications application can keep track of the total amount of time per day that the MTU and each RTU spent transmitting. This information would be included in a daily communication report. A comparison of current information to historical averages for each of these units may point to future trouble spots. An evaluation of the absolute values of these data is useful if additions or other changes to the system size are being considered.

A third communications application is called "antistreaming." It is similar to a watchdog timer. At each transmitter location, the application monitors the length of time that a transmitter is keyed on. If the transmitter stays on longer than is required, the antistreaming application turns it off, usually by removing power to the transmitter. Automatic or manual recovery methods may be used to return to normal.

11-4. Some Automatic Control

Automatic control occurs when a system senses that a process variable has changed and modifies a control parameter without bringing a human operator into the decision. An example in an electric transmission system is the automatic arming of a local load-shedding device to protect a transmission line from overloading only under very specific conditions that could be detected by the SCADA system.

Remote control occurs when a decision to modify a control parameter is effected at a significant distance from the process. The operative words in these definitions of automatic and remote control are *human* and *distance*, respectively. Very often people confuse the terms in the mistaken belief that because SCADA is associated with so much expensive computer hardware it must be automatic. In fact, most early SCADA systems and a large minority of present ones are not automatic at all. They are very efficient remote control and remote data-gathering systems. Intervention in the form of human decisions is usually required before the data that is gathered can be translated into a control action.

The increased reliability of communications networks and the increased speed and power of MTU computers have encouraged systems designers to undertake a shift toward **automatic response**. This part of Unit 11 will discuss some of the control functions that are automatic. It will concentrate on those applications that have historically been handled by the MTU. The last unit of this book, Unit 14, will discuss new and future potential applications.

Those processes that are spread over dozens or hundreds of square miles, but are not otherwise technically complex and are not likely to increase the risk to process or personnel, are better candidates for automatic control applications. In the pipeline industry, simple volume-balance leak detection had the potential to automatically block the line and shut down the pumps or compressors. Early attempts to use this automatic control were often frustrated, however, by false shut-ins with the result that most systems reverted to alarming in a control room so a human operator could make the decision. The operator's decision to block and shut down would be executed by remote control. The factors that caused false alarms were addressed by better communications and algorithms, and the tide drifted back toward automatic control for these functions.

Starting pumps or compressors in response to sensed or anticipated demands is another potential automatic control application. This also is not a very common application. Many more pump or compressor stations are controlled by local loops and/or by the remote control of human operators than by MTU automatic control. The two analogous processes in electric power transmission also qualify for automatic control through the MTU. Operating switches through the MTU in response to the situation on the entire network has become more common as network complexity increases. Small electric power generators, for example, hydro stations or wind turbines, are frequently started or stopped in response to loads. Few other applications lend themselves to true automatic control through the MTU.

11-5. Advisory Applications

If SCADA systems are not used for automatic control, what kind of control are they used for? It turns out that almost all control applications in SCADA systems bring the operator into the loop. They do this by gathering data, sometimes very large amounts from many locations over a wide geographical area; integrating it; and making it digestible by the operator. They then present it as advice. These advisory applications recognize that the operator has a better knowledge of the myriad factors that will affect the operation that the MTU simply does not know.

Many pipeline leak detection applications have the MTU warn the operator that there is probably a leak. If the operator knows that the meters are being calibrated that day, he or she may not make the decision to shut in the line. Increased demands on a product delivery system, such as an electric transmission line, may cause the MTU to advise that a particular generating facility be started up. If the operator knows that the facility is undergoing maintenance and is not available, he or she will choose another solution. For these reasons the SCADA system is used for most of these control applications as an advisory tool rather than as an automatic control tool.

Exercises:

11-1. *Some applications of SCADA require much effort and design to increase the MTU's scanning speed. Why is this important?*

11-2. *Why can it take as much as two scan periods for a field problem to be resolved if the MTU is in the decision path? What can be done to shorten this?*

11-3. *Accounting policies and government regulations sometimes control the amount of data that can be gathered electronically. What can be done to minimize billing delays?*

11-4. *Two factors determine the total price of a transferred commodity. What are they?*

11-5. *Establishing the number of units of a commodity involves two important issues. What are they?*

11-6. *What broad characteristics make an application attractive to a SCADA solution? One of them is distance; what are the other two?*

11-7. *Applications exist to monitor the communications system. Why would someone want to know the communications system failure rates on a SCADA system?*

Unit 12:
Operator Interface

UNIT 12

Operator Interface

In the last unit we learned that many, perhaps most, of the control applications that SCADA is used for involve the operator in the loop. We also discussed how SCADA gathered data and presented it so that maintenance decisions could be made. We learned that, by and large, SCADA is a hands-on tool rather than an automatic control system.

The very concept of a hands-on tool implies a requirement for fast, meaningful feedback to the operator and effective control input methods. This unit will consider the operator interface, also called the human-machine interface or the I/O (input/output). The operator interface is the junction from which information travels from the SCADA system to the operator and from the operator to the SCADA system.

Learning Objectives — When you have completed this unit, you should:

A. Understand the various ways information is presented from the system to the operator.

B. Know the various media that are available to present the information from SCADA to operator.

C. Understand how the SCADA system can be developed to make the presentation of information to the operator most effective.

D. Appreciate how operator instructions to the SCADA system can best be organized.

12-1. Security Considerations

When you consider that with a few keystrokes on a standard keyboard it is possible to shut in an entire oil field, pipeline, or electrical power system, it will be apparent that some security measures should be in place to control who makes those keystrokes. Conventional control rooms have policies in place to ensure that only those people who are authorized can effect changes. At the most basic level, there is security of access. Facilities are frequently fenced to keep the public and casual visitors from the process and the control room. Access to the control room itself is made more difficult by placing it within the fenced enclosure and then further isolating it with locks or security monitors. Within the control room and throughout the process, policies exist to allow certain groups of employees to adjust some control parameters and other groups to adjust the other parameters. Much of this procedure has carried over to SCADA. The concept of physical isolation is the first level of security. Operator interface rooms are usually located in office or control buildings and are locked and/or monitored. Only limited groups of employees can access the rooms.

Normally, data access is not further restricted. It is assumed that anyone who has accessed the room is authorized to see the data that the system is gathering. In early systems, this was a safer assumption than it is now. Modern user-friendly systems do not inherently differentiate between authorized users and unauthorized users. So much effort has been expended on making operator interfaces easy to use that computer-literate people require very little or no training to move around within the system.

Physical keylocks have been used in the past to restrict the operation of the keyboard or other operator input devices, but this was awkward, time consuming, and limiting. Current security procedures use software keys or code words to enable classes of control operations. Three classes are usually enough, but some systems provide five or more (see Figure 12-1). A process control operator would be assigned one level, which would allow him or her to adjust set points, alarm trip points, and turn equipment on or off. Instrument technicians would be assigned a different level, which would enable them to troubleshoot the communications system, access details about the frequency of various types of alarms, and adjust the assignments of alarms and other sensors. Systems engineers would be assigned a level that would allow them to access and modify the algorithms and change the accounting factors in metering calculations. The system administrator would be assigned a level that would allow him or her to assign and change code words and perform other system-level functions.

Password technology has progressed to the point where it is now practical to have the system keep track of when changes are made and by whom. This "big brother" technology is sometimes used and sometimes not, depending on the potential hazards in question and the philosophy of the operating company.

Security Level	Entitled Employees	Functions Available
A	All	—View Any Screen
B	Operator Trainees	—All "A" Functions —Change Controller Set Points —Acknowledge Alarms —Turn Equipment On or Off
C	Qualified Operators	—All "B" Functions —Change Alarm Points —Disable Controllers, Alarms
D	Instrument Technicians	—View Any Screen —Tune Controllers —Analyze All Alarm Reports —Simple Configuration
E	System Engineer	—Complex Configuration —Adjust Accounting Factors —Assign Security Codes

Figure 12-1. System with Five or More Classes of Control Operations

12-2. Alarming

Two of the economic justifications for installing SCADA are keeping the operation running and restoring it to operation quickly when it does shut down. Unit 5 described safety instrumented systems, which act to shut down a process so as to prevent injury to staff or the public, damage to the process, or negative environmental impact. In Unit 5, we also learned that these safety systems should be local. Their ability to assure safety should not depend on the communications system or the MTU.

When the protective systems do operate and shut down the process, the operator should be advised quickly so the upset condition can be rectified and downtime can be minimized. To this end, the MTU treats alarms in a special way. At the field site and in the RTU, they are treated the same way as any other status point. They exist as voltage levels on the output of a physical or electronic switch and influence the setting of a register position. But once they arrive at the MTU, they are treated differently. The condition of each point that has been identified as an alarm point is compared to its condition in the previous scan. The upper portion of Figure 12-2 shows a simple eight-bit register in the MTU that holds the condition of eight alarm points. All alarms are off except the one stored in bit 2. The lower part of the figure is the register into which the last scan information has been entered. The MTU now does a bit-by-bit comparison to check for differences. When it checks bit 1 and finds that it is the same, it does nothing except move to the next bit. When it checks bit 2 and finds that a new alarm has been generated, it goes into alarm mode. (More on that later.) When the MTU checks bit 3, it sees no change. Notice that there is an alarm there, but because it is not a change it is ignored. When it checks bit 4, the MTU sees that the alarm that had been on is now off, and it passes this information for additional processing. When it checks bits 5 to 8, it sees no change.

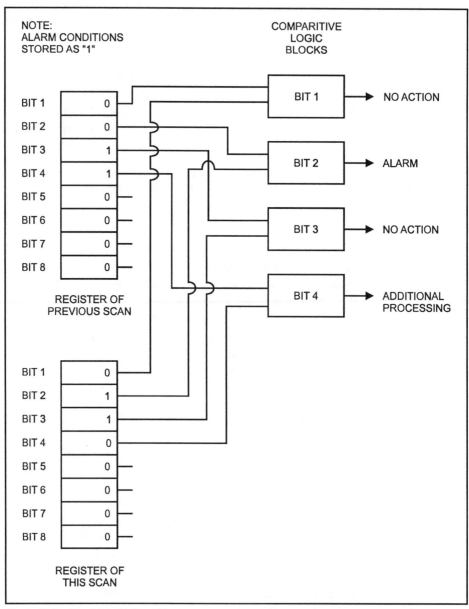

Figure 12-2. Checking for New Alarms

What has just been described is a "report-by-exception" mode. A SCADA system might monitor three thousand alarm points. If one hundred of these were in alarm (not an unusual situation) and the operator were advised of every scan, information overload would bring the system to its knees. Report-by-exception alarming tells the operator about alarms only when their status has changed.

In large systems, even that amount of information may be too much. "Alarm storms" can occur, inundating the operator with such a large series of alarm indications that he or she is overwhelmed and doesn't know how to respond. Consider the alarm regime of an unmanned oil production platform. Figure 12-3 lists four possible alarm conditions. If the generator has failed, the electrical-driven pumps will not operate, so it is not necessary to advise the operator about each one that has stopped running. The MTU can be programmed to inhibit the "Transfer Pump P101 stopped" whenever the "Generator failed" alarm is on. This is called alarm override mode. It can reduce the load during process upsets when the operator is busiest. The other two alarms in Figure 12-3 would not be overridden if they were backed up by batteries--a normal procedure for these subsystems.

Production Platform No. 1
Current Alarm Screen

- Electric Generator Failed
- Transfer Pump P-101 Stopped
- Fire in Generator Module
- Low Generator Fuel Level

Figure 12-3. Four Possible Alarm Conditions for Unmanned Oil Production Platform

Some alarm conditions are more important than others. Some cause no reaction except a comment in the next routine maintenance report. But in most SCADA systems all changes in alarm status are logged and time or date stamped. Note that the time stamp is generated by the MTU based on when it was received by the MTU. For systems with long scans, this time may be as much as one-half hour after the event actually happened. If the alarm is not being overridden it will be checked for priority. When the system is configured, each alarm is assigned a priority. There may be between one and five or more levels of priority. Figure 12-4 shows that the lowest (in this case, priority 3) would result in the alarm being printed on the dedicated "alarm screen." The second-lowest priority would cause the same result but would also cause a certain part of any screen to flash, alerting the operator to refer to the alarm screen for further information.

The highest priority would also result in the alarm being printed on the dedicated alarm screen but would sound an audible alarm as well, calling the operator to the workstation from wherever he or she was in the facility.

Alarm Priority	SCADA System Reaction
1.	Print on "Alarm Screen" Print on "Alarm Log" Flash "Alarm" on any active screen Sound audible alarm
2.	Print on "Alarm Screen" Print on "Alarm Log" Flash "Alarm" on any active screen
3.	Print on "Alarm Screen" Print on "Alarm Log"

Figure 12-4. Effects of Various Priority Alarms

Alarms must be acknowledged by the operator. When they are, the special features (flashing and sirens) go away. Generally, a return to normal on a later scan will <u>not</u> cancel these features unless the operator has acknowledged the alarm. Time-stamping the operator acknowledgment into the alarm log is normally done by the MTU.

12-3. Control Change Screens

Because the available control functions are rather limited and are often of a supervisory nature, the operator interface screens that allow these changes do not have to be complex. Figure 12-5 shows a simple control screen for a gas pipeline compressor station. Notice that for this application, and, in fact, for most control and monitoring screens, all of the points refer to equipment at one location. Notice also that most control functions can be effected by moving the screen cursor to a spot next to the devised control function and pressing the Enter button. In the case of adjustments to the speed, the appropriate speed would be entered after the cursor movement and the Enter button would be hit.

Some control screens will include an additional column to advise the operator of the present status of each control function. If this is done, some provision must be made to alert the operator that an order has been given and that the system is waiting for the next scan to confirm that the order was implemented. Starting a compressor may require a dozen or more individual actions, each one of which must be accomplished in a definite sequence and only after various conditions have been confirmed. The logic for this detailed control is located at or near the equipment. It is neither necessary nor advisable to locate it at the MTU. The SCADA operator is interested only in getting the compressor to start. After it is ordered to start, the operator wants to know if it did. If it fails to start, a message should come back telling of the failure. The operator can then send out a maintenance crew to repair the compressor.

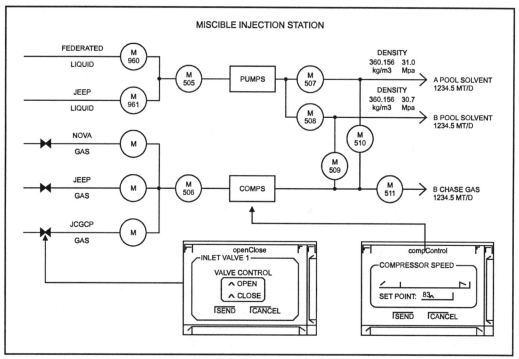

Figure 12-5. Control Screen (Courtesy: TesserNet Systems Inc.)

12-4. Status Screens

Besides knowing about status changes associated with ongoing control commands, the operator must be kept informed of the status of the many pieces of equipment under his or her control and of the many others that he or she cannot directly control. Operators responsible for manually controlled processes regularly do walkabouts. They move from area to area within the process, checking to see if the situation is as they expected it to be. A series of well-designed status screens allows operators to do an electronic walkabout. Figure 12-6 shows the diverse range of equipment status points that can be brought back. With a bit of experience, operators can become surprisingly well informed from the information contained in a small number of points.

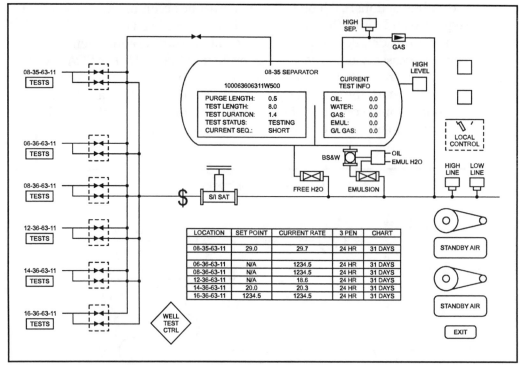

Figure 12-6. Status Screen (Courtesy: TesserNet Systems Inc.)

12-5. Graphics and Trending

In very early SCADA systems the operator interface consisted of light boxes and banks of physical toggle switches mounted in large control room panels. Recent systems use interfaces much like the ones described earlier in this unit. The low level of complexity means that monochrome computer screens that support alphanumeric messages are usually sufficient for moving the information back and forth. But in the same way that experienced operators can tell more about a process than a status screen is directly telling them, advances in color graphical interfaces allow less experienced operators to intuitively grasp the process situation faster and with less effort than with a monochrome alphanumeric interface. Color graphical operator interfaces are standard on all systems now being built.

Not only do the interfaces use color graphics, most now have the pull-down menu and the point-and-click features that have been available for years on the various "windows" packages. Most manufacturers now make systems with these capabilities. Such systems can be set up so logically that the need for formal operator training is significantly reduced. Often the benefits of providing this kind of technology cannot be anticipated.

The ability to plot data that is related in unknown ways to other streams of data can reveal patterns that change the way processes are operated.

12-6. Reports

Earlier in this unit we referred to alarm logs and communication reports. These are only two of the vast number of reports that may be required from a SCADA system. These reports may be grouped in several ways. A common grouping is preformatted versus custom or ad hoc reports. Another grouping is those that print automatically at a fixed time and those that print only when asked for, or on demand.

Most companies operating SCADA require that one printer, the alarm log printer, be dedicated to recording alarms. The same information is now routinely recorded on and held in a data historian, but data historians are perceived to be transitory. Hard copy is forever. Although many days' worth of alarm logs may never be looked at, they are available if needed and don't take up much storage space. Since the alarm log printer records each alarm, acknowledgment, and return to normal, it is usually busy and noisy. Alarm log printers are often relegated to closets or other soundproof areas near the control room.

There may be a need for routinely printed reports that the SCADA operator does not normally see. Daily communication reports, accounting-related information, and reports detailing the need for process maintenance are examples. These reports should also be printed away from the control room.

The final group of reports consists of those that the operator uses to run the facility. Examples include a special alarm report to help analyze a problem or a run report that enables each field operator to carry a hard copy detailing the recent operation on the part of the field that is his or her responsibility. The printer that produces these reports should be in the control room.

12-7. Parallel Operator Interface

In its upward spiral, computer technology has now made it possible for multiple screen/keyboard stations to be connected to one workstation. Translated into SCADA language, that means that more than one interface can be driven by one MTU.

It is seldom a problem to have more than one operator running a SCADA system. If the load exceeds the ability of one operator, the system can be split into two or three completely separate suboperations within the SCADA system. Operations that are growing or that are being updated can benefit from having the system engineer or technologist connected to the MTU. But when this is done each operation uses a separate interface and is enabled by a password or the appropriate authority to avoid interfering with the action of the operator.

This parallel operation requires that great attention be paid to enabling the various people who can access the MTU to communicate with each other. It also increases the importance of security for the system because now the system interface equipment has several physical locations.

Exercises:

12-1. *MTUs can present information to operators in two forms. What are they?*

12-2. *What is the first way in which security of a system is increased? The second?*

12-3. *Frequently, three levels of security are established, and various groups of people in the operating company can access a level appropriate to their needs. Which three levels were discussed in this unit?*

12-4. *User-friendly systems offer one disadvantage in SCADA. What is it?*

12-5. *In what way does the MTU treat an alarm point differently than it treats a status point?*

12-6. *What is meant by "reporting by exception"?*

12-7. *What is the purpose of an alarm log?*

12-8. *Why is trending, the graphic presentation of a series of data points, so effective?*

Unit 13:
SCADA Economics

UNIT 13

SCADA Economics

Several times in this Independent Learning Module we have referred to some aspect of economics. In this unit, we will concentrate on the basic economic and business factors that you should consider when evaluating whether a process can benefit from SCADA. This discussion is about economic principles rather than numbers. The costs of installation, technical support, and maintenance will vary from area to area. To do an actual economic evaluation, you will have to gather local numbers for these costs and benefits.

Learning Objectives — When you have completed this unit, you should:

A. Appreciate the methods used to quantify costs and benefits.

B. Understand the qualitative factors that must be considered to answer the question, "Should we install SCADA on this process?"

13-1. Costs versus Benefits

Reaching economic decisions may appear to be a simple process. Add all the benefits, subtract all the costs, and, if the result is positive, do it! In the real world, however, life is seldom so straightforward. The design of a SCADA system is an iterative process. Each incremental increase in system benefit (capability) creates a corresponding but nonlinear increase in cost.

If the corporation that will own the system has no existing SCADA infrastructure on which to build, the cost to get started will be high. The MTU is a large cost of the system. If they cannot be leased, communications links are also high-cost items. These parts of the system must be supplied before any benefits can accrue. The commitment and cost to a company to develop in-house expertise can be high. The large potential costs of one or two bad decisions made during the early stages of system development can exacerbate this cost. Experts in SCADA technology are available to act as consultants, but to ensure success for your job such consultants must also consider the factors that are unique to your industry or your company.

The benefits identified first tend naturally to be more valuable. For example, it may be that the cost of an all-weather road to a station can be deferred if remote control is provided. Perhaps an operating license will be contingent on the inclusion of remote shut-in capability, in which case the capital project cannot be built without SCADA.

13-2. The Time Value of Money

The discussion in Section 13-1 was presented as if the costs and the benefits would all occur on the day that the decision to implement SCADA was made. This is a convenient way to think about costs and benefits, but unless the time value of money is taken into account it can lead to wrong decisions. The story is told of the island of Manhattan being bought from the Manhattan Indians for trade goods valued at $24. Most people who hear the story feel that the purchasers got the better of the deal. It may be interesting, however, to do a quick time-value analysis.

Example 13-1. Assume that the purchase of Manhattan Island took place in 1626; the $24 was invested at 7.2 percent, compounded; and the investors paid no tax on interest. There is a rule that says that an amount of money will double when the product of interest rate times investment period equals 72. It is called, logically enough, "The rule of 72." At 7.2 percent, the investment would double every ten years ($7.2 \times 10 = 72$).

In 1626, the investment is worth $24.

In 1636, the investment is worth $48.

In 1646, the investment is worth $96.

In 1656, the investment is worth $192.

From this, a formula can be developed that states that for any year

Present Value (PV) = $24. $\times$ 2 [(present year – 1626)³ 10]

In 1726, the investment PV= $24. $\times$ 2 [(1726 – 1626)³ 10]

$$= \$24. \times 2^{10}$$

$$= \$24. \times 1024$$

$$= \$24{,}576.$$

In 1826, the investment PV= $25,165,824.

In 1926, the investment PV= $25,769,803,000.

My spreadsheet program shows that in 1996, the value is about $3.3 trillion. What we have calculated here is the present value of the investment at 7.2 percent interest, which is often written PV7.2.

When doing economic calculations, you should use the interest rates that are available to your company for investing its money. You should use a selection of these values to check whether an investment decision is sensitive to various interest rates. If your company could get 10 percent interest on an investment, you would calculate PV10, but you should also check PV7 and PV13 to see how sensitive your project is to a 3 percent change in interest rate.

In the same way that you can calculate the present value of an investment made in the past, you can determine the present value of a cost that must be paid out in the future.

Example 13-2. As part of our proposed SCADA system, we know we will have to pay $200,000 to plow optical fiber cable to three RTU sites. This payment will have to be made two years from now. We can get 10 percent interest for our money. (Ignore tax.) What is the present value cost of the optical fiber cable? (Hint: The present value of a future cost can be thought of as the amount of money that must be invested now in order to yield the cost in the future.)

We will use the common interest formula, $A = P \times (1 + i)^t$, where

A = accumulated amount

P = principal

i = interest rate/unit time (in decimal form)

t = time (in number of units)

We know that the accumulated amount is $200,000, the interest rate is 0.10 per year, and the time is two years. Transpose the equation to yield the following:

$$P = A \div (1 + i)^t$$
$$P = \$200,000 \div (1 + 0.10)^2$$
$$P = \$165,289.$$

This is the amount of money we will have to put in the budget now at 10 percent interest to have $200,000 at the time we need to plow in the cable.

The present value of a benefit that will be gained by having a SCADA system can be calculated in a similar manner.

Example 13-3. The operations engineer for an electric power company estimates that the improved utilization of facilities made possible by a SCADA system will make it unnecessary to buy $300,000 worth of electric power every year from a neighboring power grid. The deferral of this power purchase will be possible for eight years from now. The interest rate is 12 percent. (Ignore tax.) It will take two years to build the SCADA system. What is the PV12 of this benefit?

> For year 1, SCADA system is not built. No benefit.
>
> For year 2, SCADA system is not built. No benefit.
>
> For year 3, $300,000 benefit, averaged halfway through the year.
>
> $$PV = A \div (1 + i)^t$$
> $$PV = \$300,000 \div (1.12)^{2.5}$$
> $$PV = \$225,983.$$
>
> For year 4, $PV = \$300,000 \div (1.12)^{3.5}$
> $$PV = \$201,771.$$
>
> For year 5, $PV = \$180,152.$
>
> For year 6, $PV = \$160,850.$
>
> For year 7, $PV = \$143,616.$
>
> For year 8, $PV = \$128,229.$

The total PV12 is the sum of all these amounts. PV12 = $1,040,601.

In the same way that the value of benefits received in the future must be discounted by a number related to interest, the future value of some of these items must be increased by a number related to inflation. Labor rates, for example, can be projected to rise over time in some more or less predictable manner. The cost of a commodity can be projected to increase or decrease in response to demographic demand, natural supply, and several other factors. The SCADA designer is not usually expected to originate these numbers, but he or she should be aware that they will have an effect on the economic decisions.

13-3. Capital Costs

Capital costs are the first ones considered when the word *costs* is mentioned. Indeed, they are usually significant and are usually easy to quantify. These costs normally include engineering and installation labor, the services of technical specialists, warehousing, and transportation, in addition to the costs for the hardware devices that are conventionally thought of when the term *costs* is used.

Table 13-1 is a list of those items that may be included as capital items for a SCADA project.

Location	Capital Items
Central	Design/construction engineering
	Master terminal unit (MTU)
	Control room c/w heat, light, air conditioning, and ventilation
	Security (push-button door locks)
	Furniture
	Uninterruptible power supply (UPS)
	Communications equipment (may include radios, modems, antennae, and towers)
Remote	Design/construction engineering
	Remote terminal unit (RTU)
	Marshaling/termination panels
	Uninterruptible power supply (UPS)
	Communications equipment (may include radios, modems, antennae, and towers)
	Special sensors and actuators
	Interconnection of RTU to sensors and actuators
	Building in which to house RTU/UPS/communications equipment
	Light, heat, air conditioning, ventilation
Between Central and Remote	May include capital contribution to utility for leased communications lines
	May include radio repeater stations (if owned radio)
	May include purchase and installation costs (if owned copper or optical fiber cable)

Table 13-1. Capital Items

Some items are closely related to these but qualify as "capital-related expense items." The things that might qualify include the removal of existing equipment to make room for new equipment, certain refurbishments of existing buildings or equipment, and custom-designed computer software. Different jurisdictions allow different things into the expense category. Check your local laws before you get too creative. We will discuss expense items later in Section 13-9.

13-4. Training and Maintenance Costs

For some reason, training and maintenance costs are frequently neglected during the economic cycle. It is true that training costs are not very high, but they do exist. The failure to include training in the planning stage will likely lead to the failure to schedule operators' and technicians' time for that training. To have an existing group of operators provide the manpower to configure the system you must address the issue of training for them and any related adjustments to their schedules very early in the project. The costs for the instructor and the training aids should be negotiated before the system is selected. The costs for the time lost while operators learn the system are real and should be included in the cost-benefit analysis.

Maintenance technicians will have to be trained in the equipment they will become responsible for because it will be unfamiliar to them. Their maintenance duties will begin later than the configuration duties of the operators. For this reason, their training may be deferred. On the other hand, if the maintenance technicians will be actively involved in the installation, their training may be scheduled earlier. It will be most effective if it is provided just before it is to be applied.

The best location for training courses will depend on the number of people who must be trained and the cost of travel to the facility. Regularly scheduled in-house courses may work best if only a few people are to be trained. Having the instructor travel to the site will be more cost-effective than having ten workers travel to another site. Offsetting the travel costs, however, is the value of such intangibles as having your people meet valuable sources of technical information or the status that goes with a factory trip. Moreover, the trainees' learning effectiveness will be reduced if they are interrupted by operations problems, as they may be if the training occurs at their normal work location.

Maintenance costs are high enough that they should be included in the economic evaluation. It is not the MTU and RTUs that are responsible for most of these costs, although they and the communications equipment will provide their share at the beginning. Over the life of the SCADA system, most of the maintenance costs will be for the calibration, repair, and replacement of mundane items such as flow-measuring equipment, limit switches, analyzers, and actuators. The wire terminations that join all of these components into one system are also a major source of maintenance cost. Each of the process parameters that, in a manually operated facility, could be monitored by eye or by a simple sensor will have to be monitored by a more complex sensor. Each remotely operated valve requires an actuator. All of these devices that have moving parts will wear out or break. The point is that because there are so many of them, the maintenance load will be significant. Software upgrades will also contribute to maintenance costs.

Properly designed and manufactured electronic equipment that has no moving parts can be expected to suffer high "infant mortality"; that is, it will fail near the beginning of its life and then settle down to be a low-maintenance item. This is the reason most industrial electronic equipment is delivered only after an extended "burn-in" period. Early failures are more easily accepted if they happen at the factory. With proper attention to voltage transients and over-temperature protection, RTU equipment can last more than twenty years. However, improvements in technology may make it advantageous for RTU equipment to be replaced before it stops working.

Anticipating this infant mortality, you may plan to have most of the maintenance base load handled by company technicians and the initial extra load handled by people contracted specifically for that purpose. Warranties may meet both these needs. You may also want to contract some (or all) of the specialty work, such as radio or optical fiber system maintenance. These costs should be included in the economic calculations for the project.

13-5. SCADA Operating Costs

Besides system maintenance costs, the size of your operating costs will vary with the size of the system. For all but the largest systems, energy costs and consumables in the form of report paper and backup media are negligible. The cost of manpower in the form of operating staff may be the largest nonmaintenance cost. The size of this operating staff will depend on the system's size and complexity as well as its operating philosophy. Some simple irrigation systems may operate essentially unmanned, with only one operator checking in once or twice during a single eight-hour shift. Large systems in electric utility transmission or generating service may require six or more operators per shift with two or three shifts per day.

For systems that use leased telecommunications services, the cost of such leasing must be factored into the economics. These costs may represent the largest operating cost. Such operating costs should be included in the economic planning phase.

13-6. Benefits: Reduced Capital Costs

Finally, after discussing all the increased costs that are attributable to the SCADA system, we now consider some of the benefits. One potential benefit of SCADA that should be evaluated is the reduction in capital costs of the entire facility, including process and SCADA, that it makes possible. Opportunities to capture these reduced capital costs should be vigorously pursued. For many processes, they will simply not exist. For others, the value of these reduced capital costs can easily offset the entire capital cost of the SCADA system. The process of identifying opportunities for capital cost reduction should be performed by a multidisciplinary team that includes operations, construction, and maintenance people.

Table 13-2 lists some examples of cost reduction projects with the order-of-magnitude capital cost savings they make possible.

Industry	Item	Dollar Savings
Offshore	Eliminate living quarters on platform.	$1,000,000
Irrigation	Eliminate all-weather road to metering site.	$250,000
Electric transmission	Eliminate all-weather road to switching site.	$400,000
Gas pipeline	Eliminate living quarters at compressor station.	$300,000

Table 13-2. Capital Cost Savings

13-7. Benefits: Reduced Process Operating Costs

This category of benefits includes the largest number of items. Most are of small value relative to the capital costs we reviewed earlier. When added up, however, they often provide sufficient incentive to justify the installation of SCADA. A multidisciplinary team with a strong background in operations will be the most effective at identifying and quantifying them.

The time operations people spend, either traveling to or from a site or ineffectively on site, often represents a large amount of value. The benefits SCADA offers in reducing this time cost will be enjoyed most by widely scattered locations that have only a few process measurements and/or controls at each site. That is why SCADA has made such inroads in this type of facility. But, besides savings in salaries, the operations specialists will also identify other related benefits from SCADA. It may reduce the capital and maintenance costs of vehicles, overtime paid for off-shift call-outs, road maintenance costs, and a host of other things that may apply only to the industry or facility being evaluated. These determinations are best made by the operations specialists.

A properly instrumented facility with SCADA capabilities can have its protective systems set to shut down equipment earlier than would a non-SCADA facility. It can do this because operations knows that the shutdown will be recognized quickly and there will be less downtime as a result. The benefits from this are twofold: the facility may be safer and more environmentally benign, and long-term machine maintenance costs will probably be lower with faster shut-ins. The record keeping of machine failures and maintenance costs can be more effective on SCADA-equipped processes, leading to reduced preventive maintenance expenses.

13-8. Benefits: Improved Facility Effectiveness

Large amounts of capital are spent on facilities that depend on SCADA. Hydroelectric or wind-powered generating stations, offshore oil platforms, and gas compression stations all have capital costs in the millions of dollars. This money has been spent with the understanding that SCADA will provide a return while it is operating. Maximizing the amount of time that a facility runs is one of the largest benefits SCADA systems can provide.

An oil well in an onshore field may be visited once a day. If it stops producing five minutes after the operator leaves, it may be twenty-four hours before the failure is discovered. A compressor station's failure could be inferred by reduced pressure or throughput at the next manned site, but it may be a long time before the operator can drive to the station and fix the problem. The continuous monitoring available through SCADA would identify such failures immediately, thus making it possible to minimize their impact.

These are the modes of facility effectiveness that SCADA systems can address. Working together, operations, maintenance, and design engineering teams will find many more. Quantifying them and then converting the benefits into present value form will make it possible to bring them into the economic equation.

13-9. Tax Implications

For most of the examples noted in this unit, we ignored tax when we did the calculations. One of the reasons for this was that it simplifies the calculations. The other is that methods for calculating tax vary from one country to another and from one industry to another within each country.

When you do the calculations for a real project, however, you cannot ignore the role of tax in the economics of a decision. Because it is such a broad field (and because it has very little to do with SCADA), we will not discuss tax beyond this statement: Ensure that each benefit and each cost in the economic evaluation has had the appropriate tax treatment applied to it. To do this, you will need the services of a person who is a specialist in the local tax rules for the industry in question. Many operating companies develop and maintain comprehensive economic models into which the costs and benefits can be fed in order to determine after-tax effects.

Exercises:

13-1. *What two basic factors make up the economic equation?*

13-2. *Why should the time value of money be significant?*

13-3. *Why is a taxation specialist needed for SCADA economics?*

13-4. *What is meant by the present value of a cost to do something in the future?*

13-5. *The benefits associated with reduced project capital cost should be taken into account early. Why?*

13-6. *What group of people will be best able to identify potential operating savings?*

13-7. *In addition to direct costs for training, what other aspect of training is important?*

13-8. *How can SCADA improve facility effectiveness?*

Unit 14:
What's Next?

UNIT 14

What's Next?

SCADA systems consist of three functional components: communications equipment, remote terminal units (RTUs), and master terminal units (MTUs). It is reasonable to ask what changes we may expect these components to undergo in the near future. Some of the advances identified in this section are in fact already available as this book goes to press, but because they have been discussed very little or not at all we will discuss them in this unit.

Besides the communication between RTUs and MTUs, another plane of communication is starting to evolve that promises to shift SCADA from primarily a remote control tool to a truly automatic system.

Learning Objectives — When you have completed this unit, you should:

A. Know how hardware advances in communications and electronic packaging are likely to affect the future of SCADA.

B. Know how computer software advances, particularly those related to data presentation and to high-speed data transfer, will affect SCADA systems.

14-1. Better Communications

Throughout this Independent Learning Module we have emphasized that communications is the spine of SCADA technology. All information from remote sites must successfully negotiate the communications system to get from the RTU to the MTU. It has probably been obvious that, like the human spine, most SCADA communications backbones will give you serious problems at some time during their lives. They are better now than they were, but they will be better in the future than they are now.

The electronics of radio communications is benefiting from advances in other electronics technology. Packaging and fabricating methods, for example, are able to reduce the frequency drift caused by thermal changes. System reliability or availability is also being increased because designers have a better knowledge of the effects of heat and vibration and are able to do things to reduce both. Radio equipment can now be built smaller and it uses less power, making it possible to integrate it with its modem equipment right into the RTU. The ability to do this type of integration at the remote site often makes the difference between being able to provide an environmentally controlled (heated) enclosure and just keeping the rain off.

Radios are also becoming more sophisticated in their ability to monitor, maintain, and calibrate themselves. Digital accessories built into existing radios allow maintenance personnel to set up radios without the mass of hardware that was once necessary. Equipment is becoming available that will calibrate itself. Radios now being developed as integrated parts of an RTU, modem, and radio package will be able to make more effective use of scan time. As a result, they will waste less time stabilizing after transmitter turn-on than they do now. It is difficult, but not impossibly difficult, to design radios with transmitter stabilization that is measured in milliseconds. When radios were designed for person-to-person communication, the benefits of such short stabilization could not offset the increased design and construction cost. For equipment that is specifically designed to be used in SCADA, however, these benefits are now perceived to be worth the effort.

Earth satellite communications has been used for decades to move large amounts of telephone and data information. Until recently, communications satellites were designed to receive information from only a limited number of ground stations, and the cost of building two-way ground stations was prohibitively high. That is changing now, and satellite links are becoming affordable. Long pipelines and resource extraction facilities in topographically rough country will benefit from the fact that a geosynchronous satellite 36,000 kilometers away may be easier to talk to than a UHF radio receiver as little as 20 kilometers away. Figure 14-1 shows how the satellite is used as a repeater to overcome the line-of-sight limitation that UHF radio communications imposes.

Several companies are promoting the concept of low earth orbit (LEO) or highly elliptical orbit (HEO) satellite communication. Their advantages are that much less power are required to access the satellite. The goal of this technology is to make it possible for hand-portable ground stations to reach the satellites. The expectation is that the costs of these stations will fall to cellular telephone prices. Not only would this have profound implications for cellular telephones, it would simplify SCADA communications enormously.

Wireline communications is unlikely to undergo any advances that will cause significant changes in SCADA technology. Optical fiber technology, on the other hand, will probably change the way SCADA is applied to industry in fundamental ways. As originally conceived, SCADA was built around the very slow data rates of twisted-pair wireline and voice-band radio. The RTUs and the MTUs evolved with these limitations in mind. The entire technology was predicated on unreliable, slow, two-way data movement. As we have learned throughout this Independent Learning Module, small amounts of critical information, infrequently sampled, make SCADA what it is. Suddenly, a medium now exists that offers SCADA systems a bandwidth that for all practical purposes is unlimited. Evolution is over—the revolution begins.

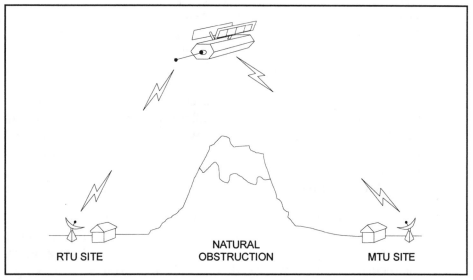

Figure 14-1. Satellite Used as a Repeater to Overcome UHF Line-of-sight Limitations

Scan periods are now limited by the electronics, not by the communications medium. Data rates are now high enough that error-correction codes or multiple transmit-and-compare techniques can assure the error-free movement of information. Security concerns involving errors in data transmission and sabotage and industrial espionage are at least partially allayed by the fact that it is difficult to break into the fiber without being detected. All of these benefits are available to most SCADA applications for a very reasonable price. Figure 14-2 provides a comparison of data rates and costs for various media.

New installations of electric power generation systems can include optical fiber in the transmission equipment. Overhead transmission cable is available that includes the fiber in an integral unit. Figure 14-3 illustrates the concept. Also commonly available is armored optical fiber cable that is suitable for burial in the same trench as new pipelines or for ploughing in the right-of-way of new or existing pipelines. Telephone utility companies have driven the cable manufacturers to perfect this configuration as a replacement for the ploughed or trenched armored copper cable. Figure 14-4 shows one manufacturer's cable construction.

Media	Data Rate bps	Capital Cost $	Lease Cost $/year
Owned Copper Cable	300-2400	6,000-20,000/km	0
Leased Telephone Cable	300-9600	0-10,000/km	~ 60/km
Owned Optical Fiber	300-10 Million +	6,000-20,000/km	0
UHF Radio	300-4800	1,000-4,000	0
Digital UHF Radio	19.2-128 Thousand	15,000	0
Earth Satellite	1200-64 Thousand	6,000-13,000	800-2400
Owned Microwave	1 Million-10 Million +	350,000	0

Figure 14-2. Comparison of Data Rates for Various Media

Because of pressure from telephone communications companies, armored underwater cable is available that allows groups of offshore platforms or subsea equipment to communicate with each other. Applications that require a high data rate can often justify the installation of optical cable. Low-data-rate sites may be more effectively served by conventional UHF radio, satellite links, or leased or dedicated twisted-pair copper cable.

Earlier we said that optical fiber technology will probably change the way SCADA is applied to industry in fundamental ways. This means that because optical fiber will remove the limitations on data rates and increase the security of the data pass, there will be a trend toward moving essentially all data from RTUs to MTUs. You might well ask, "Is the resulting system a SCADA system or a very large distributed control system?" To answer this question you may have to consider the level of the control signals being sent from the MTU. That level may affect the way the system is applied.

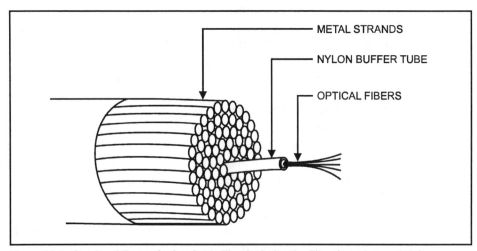

Figure 14-3. Overhead Transmission Cable That Includes the Fiber in an Integral Unit

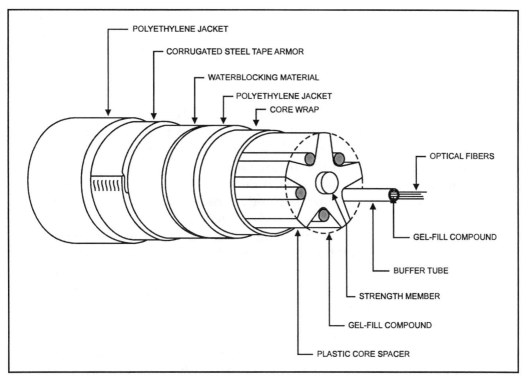

Figure 14-4. One Manufacturer's Cable Construction

14-2. Smarter RTUs

We have learned that RTUs were initially developed as electronic black boxes whose flexibility of function was controlled by adding or deleting chunks of hardware. Customer demands led to increasing flexibility to the extent that programs in assembler or higher-level languages could be written and burned into EPROMs. These programs could be accessed by the RTU controller as they were needed.

The step that is now underway is driven more by the availability of technological solutions than it is by customer demand. Miniaturization and the plummeting costs of complete personal computers are making quite sophisticated computers available for about the same price as a simple built-for-purpose RTU. Signal-conditioning cards are becoming generally available that interface between field sensors, actuators, and the computer hardware. Operating systems that allow multifunction operation permit scan response and other externally driven interrupts.

The flexibility of these computer-based RTUs will allow more functionality to reside within them. PID controllers, programmable logic controller (PLC) logic, and fluid meter totalizing can now be accomplished with these so-called smart RTUs. Very complex control, including statistical and knowledge-based methods, will also eventually become available. One potential concern regarding smart RTUs is the "all your eggs in one basket" issue: If there is a failure of any of a number of components in a smart RTU, the likelihood exists that *all* control and data gathering will be compromised.

The same concerns existed when direct digital control (DDC) was introduced to process control. And it is likely that the same solutions reached then will be used to allay smart RTU concerns as well, that is, redundancy and more attention to safety systems. Integrating functions within one module makes a big difference in installed cost. The effort needed to design machine-machine interfaces is forestalled, the labor of making the physical connections is not required, and smaller enclosures and power supplies can be exploited. These savings can be used to pay for the redundancy, graceful degradation, and self-diagnostics that will be demanded by customers and required by regulation. These savings can certainly offset the additional cost of replacing cheap disposable computers with industrial-grade models.

One note of caution must be inserted here. Smart RTUs appear to be able to solve the logic associated with protective instrument systems. You should overcome the temptation to use them for this purpose. A detailed risk analysis, which also details the probability and consequences of failure, should be performed before any protective shutdown is made dependent on a programmable electronic system.

14-3. Smarter MTUs

From the beginning of SCADA, MTUs have been computers. As MTUs become more powerful and cost-effective, they can have more functionality built into them and can form the basis of SCADA systems that could not have previously passed the economic justification hurdles. The functionality of smarter MTUs in the future will expand on three fronts. We can expect to see better operator interfaces, more stand-alone automatic control, and better machine-machine communication.

Operator control is becoming more effective. The analysis of operator response has led to better displays and has made the responses easier to initiate. Graphical user interface (GUI) tools developed for other technologies are being incorporated into SCADA. Windows environments enabled by the more powerful MTUs will or already have become standard. Massive banks of fast memory will permit object-oriented graphics control and status screens that present operators with large amounts of easy-to-digest information.

The ability to manipulate data and the increased amount of data that is available will lead to new presentation techniques. At present, most variables can be trended or plotted against time. In future systems, we can expect to see one process variable plotted against one or more other process variables. Knowledge-based systems will be embedded in future MTUs, resulting in truly smart MTUs. Particularly in fast processes such as electric power transmission and large processes such as pipelines, the operator is required to process great amounts of data, compare it to large numbers of contractual constraints, and develop orders to send out over the SCADA system. This regime is a natural for knowledge-based systems. The constraints are rules against which the incoming data can be measured. The outputs will, at least initially, be presented as recommendations for the operator to act upon.

Automatic control will increase when these knowledge-based applications enable direct control rather than merely providing recommendations. Confidence will have to be developed through successful experience, but the benefits in some applications will be sufficient to ensure that the technology succeeds. In addition, automatic control using conventional algorithms is likely to increase. It has been recognized for some time that a really large operation could be treated like smaller processes, but the computing power required to do it was not available in the MTU. Transferring the data out of the MTU and solving the control algorithm on a batch basis was the alternative. This approach was effective, but because of the difficulty and time involved in transferring the data it was often not done. Also, the fact that the operator had to get involved to effect the changes meant that the process was not "automatic" control.

MTUs that have enough computing power to solve these multi-input algorithms will make this type of automatic control much more realizable.

14-4. Local Area Networks (LANs)

MTUs that have the ability to communicate over LANs offer several very valuable benefits. The MTU has historically been the controller of the SCADA system, but it has also passed two kinds of information upward to business or corporate computers: historical data and accounting information. The data pass has been slow and awkward, with the result that only limited amounts of information were passed.

Historical data was one of the types of data that has been shunted upward for storage. Because SCADA is a real-time system, it has not usually been equipped with much of a data historian or database. Many systems keep running averages or daily totals of limited data types for seven to fourteen days in the event that upward data passes are unsuccessful. This allows time for extensive troubleshooting without the loss of any data. But the lack of a historical base has meant that MTUs have limited trending ability.

We can expect all that to change now that MTUs can use LANs to store and access data in process databases. Databases located outside the SCADA system can be justified on the basis of benefits deriving from the optimization of the overall process. The proper design of these databases will allow other disciplines, in addition to SCADA operators, to access the information contained in them. Such design, together with LAN connectivity, will also allow SCADA operators to access process and equipment information that has previously been unavailable via the MTU. Combined with improved operator interfaces, this data will make the operation of future SCADA systems much more powerful than those existing today. The base data, which is vital to the continued operation of SCADA, will continue to reside in the MTU.

LANs will allow more than one operator to interface with SCADA simultaneously. Multiple operator terminals located in different rooms, even in different buildings, are presently being used, and most sophisticated systems that are being planned will include this feature!

14-5. External Applications

In the future, SCADA-related technology will move toward the distribution of the computing power among several computers, with all of them drawing from and contributing to a common database and all linked by a high-speed LAN. This concept, which is blocked out in Figure 14-5, shows the network with one SCADA MTU, several applications computers, and a common database. This configuration enables complex applications to run on one applications computer, drawing on data that has recently been gathered by the MTU. The data is operated on by the applications computer, and the result, perhaps in the form of a set point, is written into a different field of the database. Before the next scan, the MTU checks the database to determine if a new set point has been calculated. Finally, the new set point is sent out to the appropriate RTU.

Having these applications reside in external computers offers the advantage of flexibility. In the same way that we now let most knowledge-based applications only advise, not control, we will move into these external applications cautiously as well. Maintaining physical isolation provides a comfort zone.

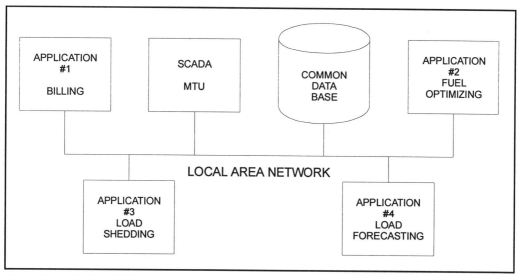

Figure 14-5. SCADA MTU Linked to Applications Computers and a Common Database by a LAN

Exercises:

14-1. *What are the three functional components of SCADA?*

14-2. *What improvements in radio communications are likely to affect SCADA the most?*

14-3. *How can satellite repeaters affect communications from RTUs?*

14-4. *What fundamental change may be made possible by optical fiber communication?*

14-5. *Name three benefits to RTUs of integrating the functions of auxiliary equipment into the RTU.*

14-6. *There are three directions in which improved MTU functionality is likely to move. What are they?*

14-7. *Large databases are becoming available that store data not only from SCADA but also from other operating and maintenance systems. Will this result in all data being retained outside the MTU?*

14-8. *It has proved feasible to use external computers to supervise MTUs. What is the significance of this for future SCADA systems?*

Appendix A:
Suggested Readings
and Study Materials

APPENDIX A

Suggested Readings and Study Materials

Independent Learning Modules

One of your best sources of material for further reading on and study of process control and instrumentation are the Independent Learning Modules (ILMs) published by ISA. They are custom designed and created specifically to provide additional information and study materials. Place a *standing purchase order* to receive new ILMs as they are published.

Practical Guide Series

ISA's Practical Guide Series (PGS) is the first comprehensive series to bridge the gap between theory and practice. The current titles available include *Control Valves* (1998), *Analytical Instrumentation* (1996), *Batch Control* (1996), *Continuous Process Control* (1996), *Maintenance of Instruments & Systems* (1995), *Statistical Process Control* (1995), *Fundamentals of Industrial Control* (1992) and *Flow Measurement* (1991).

Textbooks

ISA is the international society for measurement and control. ISA's primary goal is to provide educational materials and services to its members. Visit ISA Online at www.isa.org to purchase books, software, videos, standards, and more! At ISA Online, you'll find the latest publications, training tools and other measurement and control resources that will help you do your job more efficiently and more economically.

Appendix B:
Glossary of
SCADA Terminology

APPENDIX B

Glossary of SCADA Terminology

The definitions presented in this appendix are taken from three sources. The first is ISA's Standard on Process Instrumentation Terminology (ISA-S51.1/1984). This ISA standard contains many terms beyond the field of process instrumentation as well as many notes and amplifying figures that illuminate the terminology. The serious student of process control should have a copy of this ISA standard for routine reference. The terms in the following glossary that are defined based on this standard are followed by a "T."

Other terms have been defined using ISA's *Dictionary of Measurement and Control, 3rd Edition* (1995). This reference guide contains definitions of over eleven thousand terms and abbreviations and is the only comprehensive dictionary of measurement and control terms. The words that are defined here based on this document are followed by a "D." Finally, several terms that do not appear in either of these documents, primarily acronyms, are based on their use in the Independent Learning Module or are taken from *Webster's Dictionary*, third edition. These terms are not otherwise identified.

actuator (D) — A fluid-powered or electric-powered device that supplies force and motion to a valve closure member.

advisory — Having the power to advise.

algorithm (D) — A prescribed set of well-defined rules or processes for solving a problem in a finite number of steps.

aliasing (D) — A particular problem in data sampling where the data is not sampled enough times per cycle, and the sampled data cannot be reconstructed.

AM — Amplitude modulation (see also *modulation*).

analog (T) — Referring to "a variable which may be continuously observed and controlled."

baud (D) — A unit of signaling speed that is equal to the number of code elements per second.

bps (bits per second) — The rate of digital data transmission.

CCITT (T) — Consultative Committee on International Telephony and Telegraphy.

CPU (D) — Central processing unit.

CRC (D) — Cyclic redundancy check.

CRT (D) — Cathode ray tube.

discrete — Consisting of distinct parts. In SCADA, a signal that is either a one or a zero.

displacer (D) — A device for determining liquid level by means of force measurements on a cylindrical element partly submerged in the liquid.

duplex (D) — A method of operation for a communication circuit wherein each end can simultaneously transmit and receive.

EPROM (T) — Erasable programmable read-only memory.

flip-flop (D) — A bistable device.

FM — Frequency modulation (see also *modulation*).

geosynchronous — Moving at the same speed as the Earth does so as to remain fixed above a point on the equator.

HEO — Highly elliptical orbit. Referring to an Earth satellite that has an orbit that brings the satellite close to Earth at some point on each of its orbits. The advantage of HEO from a communications viewpoint is that much less transmitter power is required to communicate successfully when two objects are close together.

I/O (D) — A general term for the equipment used to communicate with a computer and the data involved in that communication.

ISO — International Organization for Standardization.

iterative (D) — Referring to "repeatedly executing a series of operations until some condition is satisfied."

LAN — Local area network.

LEO — Low earth orbit. Referring to Earth satellites, an orbital path that has the advantage of enabling a satellite to communicate with an Earth station with little transmitter power.

LSB — Least significant bit. In a digital word, the bit that represents the smallest value.

medium — The physical material or method between devices that are communicating.

modem (D) — An acronym for **mo**dulator-**dem**odulator.

modulation (T) — The process whereby some characteristic of one wave is varied in accordance with some characteristic of another wave.

MSB — Most significant bit. In a digital word, the bit that represents the largest value.

MTU — Master terminal unit. In SCADA, the device that acts as the master in the communications network.

OSI — Open Systems Interconnection. A nonproprietary standard model that attempts to standardize end-to-end computer communications.

protocol (D) — A set of rules and formats that determines the communication behavior of an entity.

PSK — Phase-shift keying. A modulation method that transfers information by changing the phase of the carrier wave rather than the amplitude or frequency.

real time — (D) Pertaining to the performance of a computation during the actual time that the related physical process transpires so the results of the computation can be used to guide the physical process.

refraction — The bending of a ray of light, heat, or sound when it passes from one medium to another medium whose speed of propagation differs from the first.

register (D) — In data processing, the specific location of data in memory.

RTU — Remote terminal unit. In SCADA, the device that is located away from the central control area and that communicates between the master terminal unit (MTU) and the field devices.

SCADA (D) — Supervisory control and data acquisition.

scan (D) — To sample, in a predetermined manner, each of a number of variables intermittently.

sensor — The element that receives information about the process and converts it to a form that is usable by the control system.

simplex (D) — A method of data transmission whereby the data is transmitted in one direction only.

supervisory control (T) — Control in which the loops operate independently and are subject to intermittently corrective action.

totalizer — A device that receives pulses or other basic signals and applies them to an algorithm to determine the amount of product that has been measured. It often outputs its results in engineering units.

UPS (D) — Uninterruptible power supply.

UHF — Ultrahigh frequency. Any frequency between 300 MHz and 3000 MHz.

VDU (D) — Video display unit.

Appendix C:
Solutions to
All Unit Exercises

APPENDIX C

Solutions to All Unit Exercises

UNIT 2

2-1. SCADA is different from other control and monitoring systems in that the distance between the process and the controller is normally much greater in a SCADA system.

2-2. Those SCADA systems that do operate at low data rates have a wide selection of communications media from which to choose. The option of using complex, higher-speed media is there, but cheaper, more available media can also be used.

2-3. The three primary subsystems are the MTU; its related equipment, the RTUs; and the communications equipment.

2-4. Land lines, in the form of copper or optical fiber, are one medium of communication; the other is radio in any of its many forms.

2-5. Processes are apparent candidates for SCADA if they (1) cover a large amount of space, measured in kilometers or square kilometers, (2) can be controlled by relatively simple instructions and monitoring, and (3) require frequent, regular, or fast response in order to operate well.

2-6. All of the data types mentioned can be gathered on a SCADA system by selecting end devices properly and configuring the system properly.

2-7. In almost all cases, the RTU provides electric power to the sensor, which modifies the power in some way. The sensor most commonly controls the current between 4 and 20 mA, but it may also cause the supplied power to resemble a pulse train or to be turned on or off, as in the case of a switch. In a few cases, such as thermocouples and turbine meters, the end device itself supplies the electric power, but these sensors are exceptions.

2-8. RTUs depend on electrical power to operate and to allow them to send their messages to the MTU. An uninterruptible power supply (UPS) allows the equipment that it supplies to continue to operate when normal or utility power has failed. This is often the point when the parameters that the RTU is monitoring become most important. RTUs and MTUs are often provided with UPSs to increase their reliability during power upsets.

UNIT 3

3-1. Although two-way control and monitoring did exist in limited applications before the 1960s, it was in the early part of that decade that it became a recognized technology.

3-2. The three factors are as follows: (1) The cost of installation is frequently less for radio than it is for the alternative, (2) equipment can be moved or recovered if the RTU site is discontinued, and (3) radio paths are relatively immune to the condition of the ground between the sites as well as to damage caused by construction equipment and animals.

3-3.   The other reason electronic computers replaced built-for-purpose MTUs is that the cost of computers became much lower than the cost of the alternative.

3-4.   The most profound effect of using inexpensive minicomputers is that it was no longer necessary to be limited to only one MTU. MTUs could be located in the place that made the most sense from a business point of view.

3-5.   Pipelines and electric transmission lines are linear. This allowed them to be monitored and controlled through control wires, which were the most popular media of communication in the early days of the technology.

UNIT 4

4-1.   a.   Adequate. A scan rate of once per hour will identify all significant excursions of the meter.

  b.   Inadequate. During some scan periods, several customers may fill up, but only the one filling up when the system is scanning will be detected. Many will not be charged for gasoline; one will be overcharged.

  c.   Adequate. Many pipeline leaks are small, and several readings must be summed to provide filtering. A response time for small leaks on the order of forty to fifty minutes is reasonable. To provide protection against the effects of large, catastrophic leaks you may have to depend on another technology.

4-2.   a.   A ten-minute scan would work.

  b.   A one-hour scan would work.

  c.   A twenty-four-hour scan would be too long, unless the scan were arranged to occur just before the maintenance crew planned its daily activities. Even then, it would catch only those failures that occurred before the start of the day. To be effective, a scan period of one or two hours would be acceptable for detecting failures like this.

4-3.   Nothing. All systems operating with a master-slave communications protocol require that the MTU interrogate the RTU before the RTU can respond. The RTU will have to wait until it is asked to report.

4-4.   One RTU in a group of RTUs being scanned can be addressed twice or more in each scan. This will have the effect of scanning that RTU at a higher rate.

4-5.   Most SCADA systems communicate at between 300 and 9600 bits per second (bps). This is changing as a result of the need by electric utilities and pipelines to scan large numbers of points very quickly. Many new SCADA systems, including but not limited to those used with electric utilities, are using data rates on the order of millions of bits per second.

4-6.   The following detract from the time available to communicate process data: communications overhead in the form of RTU addresses included in the message, error-detecting and -correcting codes, and radio transmitter settling times. One additional inefficiency for communications paths that are subject to noise is that some messages will be corrupted by the noise and will have to be discarded.

4-7. Scan interval cannot be determined simply by knowing the communications media. Other factors, for example, the number of RTUs being scanned and the amount of information that each RTU contributes, are also important. In general, dedicated telephone lines can support the same scan intervals as UHF radio.

4-8. a. If the separator cycle and the scan rate were each exactly two minutes, each scan would occur when the liquid level was at the same height. The level would appear to be static.

b. This would work. The liquid level would be sampled four times throughout its cycle. The operation of the separator could be inferred from this information.

UNIT 5

5-1. The independence of its elements and the fact that it is composed of few parts are the two characteristics that indicate that a SCADA system should not be used for safety instrumented systems.

5-2. Yes. Analog signals such as this are frequently monitored by SCADA.

5-3. No. The failure of the displacer would then not only inhibit the operation of the normal control system, it would also cause the protective system to be inoperative.

5-4. Communications systems contain many parts. This in itself is not the problem; however, it does contribute to low reliability. Safety instrumented systems should be composed of elements that are known to have high reliability.

5-5. Yes. This is one of the functions that makes SCADA a valuable tool for electric utilities, and it can be thought of as a normal control operation.

5-6. Local operating equipment should be installed to protect each section of the line in the event that the remote switches do not work. These local devices constitute the safety instrumented systems.

5-7. Some regulatory agencies require that billings for product delivered be backed up by paper or extended memory. Make sure you check regulations before you include this function in your SCADA.

5-8. Flow totalizers must make provision for changing factors within the algorithm and even for changes to the algorithm itself. Of course, any change to the algorithm or its factors will result in a change in the reported amount of the material being measured. A hard-copy printout can provide an accounting check when an audit of the process is needed.

UNIT 6

6-1. Low-speed SCADA uses twisted-pair copper wires, either leased from the telephone utility company or installed by the company that owns the SCADA system, or it uses inexpensive two-way radio.

6-2. A sine wave can be modulated by controlling its "amplitude," by controlling its "frequency," or by controlling the "phase" or "change of phase" of the wave. These are called "amplitude modulation," "frequency modulation," and "phase-shift modulation," respectively.

6-3.   A CRC is used to determine if the message that was received is the same as the message that was sent. CRCs are used to detect errors in communication. In some cases, they can be used to locate and correct the message, but this is seldom done in SCADA. Normally, messages that are found to have errors are just ignored. Both the MTU and the RTU calculate the CRC. The receiving station compares the CRC that it calculated to the CRC that it received. If they are not the same, a communications error is assumed to have occurred. The number of bits that a CRC contains is determined by the protocol. SCADA CRCs often have sixteen bits.

6-4.   Some modulation techniques allow data to be sent at a higher bit-per-second (bps) rate than the modulation rate.

6-5.   Buried telephone cable is composed of many twisted pairs of individually insulated copper wire. To provide protection from groundwater, mechanical damage, and electromagnetic noise, jackets, armor, and shields are added. The cost of adding this protection is so high that the cost of adding incremental pairs is comparatively low. For this reason, cables with only a few pairs cost about the same as cables with many pairs. It costs about the same amount to bury a cable with many pairs as it does to bury a cable with one pair, so buried telephone cables often have many extra pairs available. Manufacturers have developed standard configurations for the cable they make.

6-6.   The RTU that receives an analog signal must convert that signal to a string of bits, which are either one or zero. It does this with electronic circuitry called an analog-to-digital converter, sometimes called an ADC. The string of bits is stored in a register in the RTU until the MTU requests the data. The RTU then puts together a message, which includes this data, and sends it over the communications system in serial form to the MTU.

6-7.   A protocol driver arranges the outgoing message or decodes the incoming message, according to a preestablished pattern. This pattern has established the meaning of each and every bit, and the protocol driver ensures that the information that is to be communicated fits into the message in the correct location.

6-8.   One of the functions of the modem is to monitor the communications medium and to advise the RTU or MTU when there is no traffic on the medium.

UNIT 7

7-1.   Telemetry systems gather information from remote locations but do not control the remote sites. For this reason, they can use simplex communication, which allows messages to travel only one way. Because it both monitors and controls, SCADA requires two-way communication.

7-2.   If the pony express system had used only one pouch for the messages, it would have been a half-duplex system because communication could have traveled in both directions but only in one direction at a time. During those periods when more than one pouch was in operation, with some being carried west at the same time as some were being carried east, the system was operating in duplex mode.

7-3.   Transmitter turn-on time is the interval between the time a radio transmitter is directed to start transmitting and the time that it has turned on, stabilized, and can be modulated in a reliable manner. Transmitter turn-on time should be minimized in a system because it uses valuable time and decreases the amount of transmit time available for passing messages.

7-4.   If one RTU transmitted continuously, no other RTU could send its information to the MTU. A local device can be added to each RTU to monitor whether the radio transmitter is on and to disable the radio if it sticks in transmit mode. Various recovery methods can be applied after this disabling, but it should be obvious that even with no recovery such a device would be beneficial. Other RTUs would be able to operate if the broken one were disabled.

7-5.   The ratio of baud rate, which is related to bandwidth, and data rate is high for these two modulation methods. It is also high for amplitude modulation, but noise problems outweigh the advantage gained with AM.

7-6.   UHF radio operates at a frequency that is high enough for the signal to be almost line-of-sight. Hills and buildings that lie between the signal's path can have large effects on the signal. The curve of the Earth creates the need for high antenna towers if a path of more than about fifty kilometers is required.

7-7.   The charged particles that interact with the magnetic field result in electromagnetic interference of the radio communication. Noise levels can be so high that in some signals all the data is overwhelmed.

7-8.   Reduction in size, reduction in power requirements, temperature compensation, resistance to vibration, resistance to power supply transients, better long-term frequency stability, ability to use low-voltage DC power, built-in self-diagnostics, and faster transmitter stabilization.

UNIT 8

8-1.   An RTU equipped with the appropriate input capabilities can gather analog values, streams of pulses or contact closures, and digitally encoded high-speed serial streams of data.

8-2.   An RTU can develop a discrete signal to turn a machine on or off, an analog signal to open or close a machine to some degree less than 100 percent, a series of pulses to operate a stepping motor to a required position, and a digitally encoded high-speed serial signal.

8-3.   A protocol driver program encodes information according to a very well-defined set of rules so that the meaning of each bit in a serially encoded word can be recovered. The protocol driver at the receiving end of the communications path uses exactly the same set of rules to decode the received serial word.

8-4.   The three fields are "message establishment," "information," and "message termination."

8-5.   The security code enables the equipment that is receiving the message to determine if any errors have been introduced into the message between its transmission and its receipt. It checks for communication errors.

8-6.   As part of the message establishment field, some protocols define how many bytes this message will contain. Some protocols have only two permissible message lengths and alert the receiver when to expect a long message. Many protocols include an end-of-message code that is transmitted at the end of each message.

8-7.   The analog-to-digital converter (ADC) is set up so that each bit in its register represents a value that is one half of the previous bit. So a one-bit register will tell if the device is on or off. A two-bit register can tell within 1 in 2^2, or 1 in 4 (which is 25 percent), what the device's position is. An eight-bit register can tell within 1 in 2^8, or 1 in 256 (which is about 0.4 percent), what the position of the device is. This would probably be adequate for any valve position sensor. A sixteen-bit register could tell within 1 in 2^{16}, or 1 in 64,000, what the device position is. That degree of precision is beyond what is needed and is well beyond the capabilities of any valve position sensor.

8-8.   Serial ports are becoming available on more and more devices because they provide a standard physical connection through which nonstandard information may be passed. Most types of information can be coded so they can be sent over the serial port. Various standard types of ports are available. The one most commonly used is RS-232D.

8-9.   Flow totalizers receive input from one or more sensors that are measuring the parameters associated with the fluid, and they apply these inputs to algorithms. The algorithms usually have fixed factors in addition to the variable factors. These fixed factors can be dialed in to the totalizer. The output of the algorithm is a number that represents, in engineering units, the amount of fluid that has passed through the totalizer. Often, other information, such as flow rate, can also be provided by the totalizer.

UNIT 9

9-1.   This statement is true for master-slave communications.

9-2.   The station that has a definition of the entire process is the master terminal unit (MTU).

9-3.   Each remote terminal unit (RTU) only needs to have a definition of everything it interfaces with. Interfaces at other RTUs or at the MTU are of no interest to an RTU.

9-4.   MTUs communicate with RTUs, with the equipment that forms the human-machine interface, and with other computers, which may include accounting machines, applications engineering workstations, and long-term storage databases.

9-5.   For a transmission-line system that has feeder lines going off at points A, B, and C, each one of which is equipped with a remotely operated switch, the program for remotely operating the switches could look like this:

1.   If a keyboard entry calling for "Open Switch A" is made, set a flag (put a 1) in the MTU register reserved for the control of this switch. Similar instructions must be made for Switches B and C.

2.   Each time a scan is ordered, check each of these registers and compare their contents to the contents of registers that tell what the present status of each switch is (1 for open; 0 for closed).

3.   If the registers are the same, send a message to the VDU that says, "Switch A is already open." Go to standby mode.

4.   If the registers are different, include an order in this scan telling the RTU at switch location A to open the switch.

5. At the next scan, check the switch status to determine that the switch did in fact open. If it did, send a message to the VDU that says, "Switch A now open." Go to standby mode.

6. If the status registers indicate that the switch did not open, resend the order to open it on the next scan.

7. At the next scan, recheck the switch status to determine that the switch did open. If it did, send a message to the VDU that says, "Switch A now open." Go to standby mode.

8. If it did not open, send a message to the VDU that says, "Switch A failed to open." Go to standby mode.

9. For each of the three switch locations, provide a "Max Current" register in the MTU that will store the allowable current through that feeder line.

10. For each of the three switch locations, on each scan monitor the current being drawn through the feeder line.

11. Compare the value detected to the value in the "Max Current" register. If the value detected is equal to or greater than 90 percent of the value in the "Max Current" register, send a message to the VDU and to the alarm log that says, "Load on Line A is approaching critical."

12. If the value detected is equal to or greater than 100 percent of the value in the "Max Current" register, set the flag to open the appropriate switch, and send a message to the VDU that says "Switch A has been ordered to open." Send a message to the alarm log that says "Overcurrent at Feeder Line A."

13. Check the next scan to determine that the switch did open. If it did, send a message to the VDU that says, "Switch A is now open." Go to standby mode. If it did not, send another message to the RTU telling Switch A to open, and so on.

14. Apply similar logic to Switches B and C.

9-6. The ability of the MTU to transfer large amounts of information to a computer that is not directly involved with the day-to-day operation will probably cause much of this information to be stored out of the MTU. This reaction or response, however, will depend on the conjunction of communications technology like local area networks (LANs) and SCADA systems becoming common.

9-7. Graphics have the effect of increasing the need for memory for two reasons. First, graphics themselves use a significant amount of memory. Second, the ability of operators to interpret much larger amounts of data made it beneficial to have much more operating data stored in locations that were accessible to the MTU. This has created a very large demand for memory.

9-8. One of the most important things that the MTU does is to routinely run applications programs. An example of an applications program is the scanning function. Another is the process of determining whether a point is in alarm by comparing the present reading of that point to a selected value that is entered by the operator and stored in the memory registers of the MTU.

UNIT 10

10-1.   Patents are issued to allow the developer of a patented device a period of time during which he or she is protected from competition. When this period expires, others can build and market the device, and the consequent competition usually results in lower cost.

10-2.   Electric wire has been the preferred medium for moving measurement data and instructions between the process and the control room. Other media have been used, for example, compressed air and even mechanical force and motion. Electric signals have the advantage of being clean, flexible, and relatively safe. The preference for electrical media moved to RTU and process connections as an evolutionary step.

10-3.   Oil and gas processing, as well as some chemical processes, create the possibility that a process fluid will be released that can form a flammable or explosive mixture with the air. Electrical sensors must be built in such a way that they cannot ignite such a combustible mixture.

10-4.   Marshaling panels have as their primary purpose the termination of cables and wires from the process at some point near the control panel. In addition, they can be used to rearrange or reorder control signals; to mount barriers, fuses, and isolating switches in the control and monitoring circuits; and to mount instruments and indicators between the process and the main control panel.

10-5.   Often, the layout of a process results in a concentration of instruments and/or actuators. Rather than use one small cable to connect each instrument to the RTU, the designer will find it less expensive to run a multipair cable to a location near the instruments. The way the instruments are constructed precludes running the multipair cable through the instrument. A field termination box serves as the termination for the multipair cable, and from there individual cables are run to the instruments.

10-6.   Engineering charges are higher for SCADA projects because SCADA projects are composed of very large numbers of complex, but not very expensive, elements. The effort to ensure that all the parts go together properly costs a significant amount of money; the purchase and installation of the parts is also expensive but often not as much as for other capital projects. The result is that for SCADA projects, engineering costs may be as high as 50 percent of the total project cost.

10-7.   The four factors are as follows:

1.   The installation details for each type of device would have to be documented.

2.   Training would be required for operation and maintenance personnel for each type.

3.   Spare parts would have to be maintained for each type.

4.   Checkout and calibration procedures would have to be developed, learned, and maintained for each type.

10-8.   SCADA installations have many electronic parts and many electrical connections. Both of these types of equipment are subject to high initial failure. Note that when electronic equipment is burned in at the factory, fewer problems should result. With better wire termination techniques, electrical connections should cause fewer problems.

UNIT 11

11-1.   The response time of a SCADA system is directly related to the time the MTU takes to scan each RTU. The most effective way to reduce response time is to reduce scan time. Also, if additional functions or additional RTUs are being considered, an effort must be made to reduce the amount of scan time per RTU just to maintain the system response.

11-2.   If the problem occurs at an RTU just after the MTU has interrogated that RTU, it will be almost one scan period before the MTU learns of it. Using normal scan procedure, the MTU will not send its instructions to that RTU until the next regularly scheduled scan. Certain high-priority alarms or out-of-limit conditions could trigger a priority scan procedure in the MTU, which would provide instructions to those RTUs that had the specific alarm.

11-3.   Billing is often done on the basis of the electronically gathered data with the understanding that audits of the results may require changes to the billing after the fact.

11-4.   The two factors that determine price are unit cost and number of units.

11-5.   Establishing the number of units to be measured involves the issues of accuracy and security.

11-6.   The processes that are often attractive to a SCADA solution require frequent, periodic, or immediate visits so some parameter of the process can be adjusted or monitored. The types of adjustments that are required are relatively simple.

11-7.   Communications systems, like all systems, degrade over time. Monitoring them and trending failure rates can allow corrections to be made and calibration to be performed before the total failure of the system occurs.

UNIT 12

12-1.   MTUs can advise the operator by means of the VDU or CRT screen or by a hard-copy method such as a printed alarm report.

12-2.   The first level of security is called "access control." People who have no need to get close to the process or process control are physically kept away. The second level is to have a key, either hardware- or software-based, that must be used to get to the part of the system that allows control changes to be made.

12-3.   The process control operators, the instrument maintenance technicians, and the systems or control engineers were identified as examples of three levels of security.

12-4.   User-friendly systems are designed to make understanding system operation very easy. This is positive insofar as it relates to access by authorized personnel. It is negative with respect to security. Unauthorized people can often deduce how to enter and adjust user-friendly control systems that they have no business entering and adjusting.

12-5.   Changes in status at the MTU level do not trigger major reactions. They result in updates to status registers and do not cause interrupts. Alarm point changes result in the same type of register updates, but they also cause interrupts that often involve audible alarms, messages to alarm printer logs, and the need to acknowledge them.

12-6.   Reporting by exception causes a message to be sent to the operator only when an alarm situation changes. An alarm would be generated after the first scan that detected a high level in a reservoir, but after that the operator would be advised only when the level returned to normal. This method of reporting reduces the load on the operator.

12-7.   An alarm log is a hard-copy printout of all alarms, acknowledgments, and returns to normal, complete with their time of occurrence. It is automatically generated by a system. It provides an auditable record of the out-of-limits operation of the system.

12-8.   Trending uses the pattern-recognition part of the brain to evaluate large amounts of data in a relatively painless way. If a pattern exists, a graphical display like trending will allow it to be found much more easily than will table- or list-based displays.

UNIT 13

13-1.   The two basic factors that make up the economic equation are costs and benefits.

13-2.   As long as interest rates exceed 0 percent, the time value of money will be significant. One dollar in your hand today is more valuable to you than the promise of one dollar five years from now.

13-3.   Each political area establishes a taxation regime to meet its needs. Within that political area, different industries may be treated differently. Levels of taxation can make the difference between a project being economically positive or negative. Only with good advice on taxation can you accurately determine the economics of a project.

13-4.   If money must be spent to do something in the future, resources must be allocated now so that the money will be available when it is needed. These resources can be invested now, and they will grow by an amount that depends on the interest rate they are invested at and the length of time over which they are invested. The present value of the money is the amount of resources that must be invested now so the investment grows to equal the money that is needed.

13-5.   Often this class of benefits is large, and since these benefits occur early in the project life they have a high present value.

13-6.   Operations specialists are the best qualified to identify the potential operating savings of a project.

13-7.   The time at which the training is scheduled is important. Training should be provided just before the ability is needed. Other considerations involving the location of the training are also important.

13-8.   There are many ways that SCADA can improve the effectiveness of a facility. Only by conducting a comparative study of the way the facility would be operated with and without SCADA, using several different types of specialists, can an estimate be made to quantify the net benefit. Reduced capital cost, reduced operating cost, improved product quality, improved throughput, and improved response to changing conditions are a few of the factors to consider when doing such an evaluation.

UNIT 14

14-1.   Communications equipment, RTUs, and MTUs are the three functional components of SCADA.

14-2.   Improvements in reliability, power consumption, size, maintainability, and transmission turn-on time will benefit SCADA systems.

14-3.   Geosynchronous satellites are in the line of sight over enormous areas. Much of the radio band that is used for SCADA requires a line-of-sight path. Using a satellite as a repeater eliminates the problems introduced by hills and the curvature of the Earth.

14-4.   Because optical fiber has a wide bandwidth communications systems that use it will probably use communications methods other than master-slave. The reliability and noise immunity of optical fiber communication may also mean that more raw data is brought to the MTU for processing and less is done at the RTU.

14-5.   The cost of providing communication between the RTU and an auxiliary device is eliminated; the cost of the physical connection, including cabling and labor to connect, is eliminated; and smaller housing and power supplies are required if the RTU takes on the functions of some of the auxiliary equipment.

14-6.   First, MTUs will improve in the area of the operator interface, with more attention being paid to graphical methods of presentation. Second, with their increased capability to compute and the operator's increased confidence in the results of their calculations, MTUs will take on more automatic functions. Third, their ability to communicate better with other machines will allow them to exchange large amounts of information very quickly, to the extent that it will be transparent to the operator where the information he or she is accessing came from.

14-7.   There is some information, such as basic applications programs and configuration data, that is of interest only to the MTU. There are no apparent benefits to retaining this information outside the MTU.

14-8.   Reliable machine-to-machine communications and applications programs that run on engineering workstations will allow SCADA systems to be supervised by other computer systems. Many of the large-scale control functions currently executed by operators will be handled automatically by networks of computer systems.

INDEX